Saints for Young Readers
for Every Day

D0096712

SAINTS

for Young Readers for Every Day

Third Edition

VOLUME 1
January–June

Written by
Susan Helen Wallace, FSP

with Melissa Wright

Illustrated by
Jamie H. Aven

Pauline
BOOKS & MEDIA
Boston

Library of Congress Cataloging-in-Publication Data

Wallace, Susan Helen, 1940–
  Saints for young readers for every day / written by Susan Helen
Wallace with Melissa Wright ; illustrated by Jamie H. Aven.—3rd ed.
    p. cm.
  Includes index.
  ISBN 0-8198-7081-1 (pbk.)
  1. Christian saints—Biography—Juvenile literature. I. Wright,
Melissa. II. Aven, Jamie H. III. Title.

  BX4653.W35 2004
  282'.092'2—dc22

                                    2004003524

Cover illustration by Elinor Kaslow

Published by Pauline Books & Media, 50 Saint Pauls Avenue, Boston, MA 02130-3491

Printed in the U.S.A.

SYR1 VSAUSAPEOILL2-2610037 7081-1

www.pauline.org

Pauline Books & Media is the publishing house of the Daughters of St. Paul, an international congregation of women religious serving the Church with the communications media.

5 6 7 8 9 10   19 18 17 16 15

Dedicated to
Venerable Maggiorino Vigolungo

Maggiorino was a teenager who lived not so long ago. He reached a hero's level of love for God and people by following his challenging slogan: "Make a little progress every day."

Known as the young apostle of the press, Maggiorino joined the newly established Society of St. Paul in his native Italy. His burning ideal shines clearly in his own words: "With the help of God, I intend to consecrate my entire life to spreading the message of Jesus through the apostolate of the media. I want to become a saint, a great saint—and soon!"

Maggiorino was just fourteen when he died, but he was ready to meet his Lord. In fact, he had written, "Heaven! Eternal happiness! This is what is waiting for me."

How to Use This Book

This book offers a story of a saint for each day. Some lived long lives; others died when they were young. Some were close to God from their childhood and teenage years. Others learned the hard way that only God can make us happy.

In these pages you will meet saints from every nation and race. They are from different centuries, starting with the early days of the Church right down to our own times. You'll come to know saintly kings and laborers, queens and housemaids, popes and priests, nuns and religious brothers. They were mothers and fathers, teenagers and children. They were doctors and farmers, soldiers and lawyers.

Saints were as different from each other as we are. They were as human as we are. They lived on this earth, experienced temptations and faced problems. They became saints because they used their will-power to make right choices and they prayed. They tried to correct their faults and they never gave up trusting in Jesus' love for them.

Don't try to read all the stories in a few days. Read them one day at a time. The saint for the day is from the current Church calendar (called the Roman Calendar). When this calendar does not present a saint on a certain day, we have chosen one that we thought you might appreciate learning about.

You might ask, "What's the difference between a SAINT and a BLESSED?" Saints are holy persons now in heaven who grew close to God while on earth. The Church declares them saints so that we can love, imitate, and pray to them. Saints can pray to God for us and help us. Persons declared BLESSED are holy people who are now in heaven. Usually the Church requires miracles obtained through their intervention. When the miracles have been carefully studied and accepted as real, the blessed are proclaimed saints. You will also find MARTYRS in this book. Martyrs are people who allowed themselves to be put to death rather than deny God or give up their Catholic faith.

A good way to use this book is to read the saint story for the day either before or after you say your morning or evening prayers. In this way, you'll be able to think about what you read during the day and try practicing the suggestion at the end of the story. (You might also want to read more biographies of the saints you especially liked.)

If you read a story a day, you'll have made many new friends in heaven by the end of the year. And they'll be more than happy to help you to become closer to God.

Please note that due to the overlapping of dates, some of the saints appear on days that are not their feast days.

Contents

JANUARY

❋

FEBRUARY

MARCH

✸

APRIL

❁

MAY

❋

JUNE

For an alphabetical listing of all the saints and blesseds
in volumes 1 and 2, see page 325.

JANUARY

January 1

Mary, Mother of God

Today we begin a new year. It's one week since Christmas Day. In the nativity scene we have at home or at our parish, we gaze at Baby Jesus in the manger just as the shepherds did so long ago. We see Mary, his mother, and Joseph, Jesus' foster-father.

Mary was the daughter of Joachim and Anne. She loved God and her Jewish religion very much. Her neighbors probably thought Mary was very ordinary. It would be God's work in her that would make her so special, so full of grace.

God chose Mary from all women to be the mother of his Son. The Lord sent the Archangel Gabriel to Mary's town of Nazareth. Gabriel asked Mary to become the mother of God's Son. Mary wanted to please God, and so she answered "yes." With her "yes," Mary became pregnant through the power of the Holy Spirit. She became Jesus' mother. Because she is the mother of Jesus, God's Son, Mary *really* is the Mother of God! What a blessing it was for Mary and her husband, Joseph, to be the ones to raise Jesus! They spent many happy years with him in Nazareth.

When Jesus was about thirty years old, he began his preaching and healing ministry. This is usually called his public life. (It seems that Joseph had died sometime before.) Mary often went with her friends to be near her Son and listen to his words. One day, she attended a marriage celebration in a town called Cana. Jesus and his disciples came too. When the wine ran out, Mary asked Jesus to do something. She wanted him to save the couple from being embarrassed in front of their guests. That's when Jesus worked the miracle of turning plain water into delicious wine!

Mary loved Jesus and believed in him. She was there when he was nailed to the cross. She received his body into her arms after he had died and was taken down from the cross. After Jesus' resurrection, Mary waited with Jesus' apostles for the coming of the Holy Spirit on Pentecost. The apostles loved her. They knew they needed more courage to be real followers of Jesus. Mary prayed for them and encouraged them. She taught them how to be disciples of her Son. Mary's feast days are special events that we celebrate throughout the year. Today we honor Mary as God's Mother by going to Mass. We can be very happy because Jesus gave Mary to us as our mother, too.

Mary's life was closely connected with the life of Jesus. To remember the events of Mary's life is to remember the life of Jesus too. Let's ask Mary to help us love her Son Jesus more each day of this new year.

St. Basil the Great and St. Gregory Nazianzen

Basil and Gregory were born around the year 329 in Asia Minor. Today we call this area Turkey. Basil's grandmother, father, mother, two brothers and a sister are all saints. Gregory's parents are St. Nonna and St. Gregory the Elder. Basil and Gregory met and became great friends at school in Athens, Greece.

Basil became a well-known teacher. But he wasn't satisfied. He felt that God was calling him to live as a monk. Basil visited monasteries in Syria, Egypt and Palestine, then moved to the wilderness and started his first monastery. The rule he gave his monks was very wise. Monasteries in the East have followed it down to our own times.

Both Basil and Gregory became priests and then bishops. They often preached about the Holy Trinity, because the errors of Arianism were confusing many people. Arianism was a teaching that denied that Jesus is God.

While he was bishop of Constantinople, Gregory converted many people with his wonderful preaching. But it nearly cost him his life! Once, a young man planned to murder him. He repented at the last moment and begged Gregory's forgiveness. Gregory did forgive him and won him over with his gentle goodness.

Forty-four of Gregory's speeches, 243 letters and many poems were published. His writings are still important today. Many people have based their writings on his.

Gregory's good friend Basil had a very kind and generous heart. He always found time to help the poor. He even invited poor people to help those who were worse off. "Give your last loaf of bread to the beggar at your door," he urged, "and trust in God's goodness." Gregory sold his inheritance to help the poor. He also built a hospital where he visited the sick.

Basil died in 379 at the age of fifty. Gregory died in 389 at the age of sixty. He is buried in St. Peter's Basilica in Rome.

Our education, time and talents are all gifts that God has given us. If we want to be like Saints Basil and Gregory, we can use these gifts to help the people around us become closer to God.

January 3

Most Holy Name of Jesus

In his letter to the Philippians, St. Paul wrote: "At the name of Jesus every knee should bend, of those in heaven and on earth and under the earth, and every tongue confess that Jesus Christ is Lord, to the glory of God the Father" (Phil. 2:10).

The name "Jesus" means "God saves" in Hebrew. This name was given to God the Son by the angel Gabriel at the annunciation. The name "Jesus" tells us who our Lord is and what he came on earth to do. Jesus came to save us, his people, from our sins. St. Peter, filled with the Holy Spirit, declared, "There is no other name under heaven given to the human race by which we are to be saved" (Acts 4:12).

In the fifteenth century, St. Bernardine of Siena promoted devotion to the Holy Name of Jesus. He preached about the power of Jesus' name and was responsible for the addition of the name Jesus to the Hail Mary: "Blessed is the fruit of your womb, Jesus."

Through the centuries, the Church has taught us to use the name of Jesus with reverence and love. In the liturgy, we end every prayer with the words, "through our Lord Jesus Christ." There is even a short prayer called *The Jesus Prayer*, which is very easy to memorize and repeat. It goes like this: "Lord Jesus Christ, Son of God, have mercy on me, a sinner." Many great followers of Jesus, such as St. Joan of Arc, have died pronouncing his name as a prayer.

We should always use the holy name of Jesus with respect. It's a very bad habit to use the Lord's name in the wrong way, and we should never do this. When we hear other people using the name of Jesus disrespectfully, we can make up for it by praying silently, "Blessed be the name of Jesus."

St. Elizabeth Ann Seton

"Mother Seton" was the name everyone knew Elizabeth by when she died on January 4, 1821, in Emmitsburg, Maryland. A life full of surprises had led to that name.

Elizabeth Ann Bayley was born in New York City on August 28, 1774. Her father, Richard Bayley, was a well-known doctor. Her mother, Catherine, died when Elizabeth was just three years old.

In 1794, Elizabeth married William Seton. He was a rich merchant who owned a fleet of ships. Elizabeth, William, and their five children had a happy life together. Elizabeth devoted her time to her family, to helping others, and to prayer. The Seton family belonged to Trinity Episcopal Church in New York City.

But soon, Elizabeth's happy life would change. First her father, whom she loved very much, died. Then her father-in-law also died, and the Seton fortune quickly dwindled. Next Elizabeth's husband Will became sick.

In October, 1803, Elizabeth brought Will to Italy, hoping the climate there might help him get better. With their oldest daughter, Anna, they journeyed by ship. But Will died shortly after their arrival. In her grief, Elizabeth prayed, "My God, I am alone in the world with you and my little ones. But you are my Father and doubly theirs."

Elizabeth and Anna remained in Italy as guests of the Filicchi family. The Filicchis were very kind. They tried to ease Elizabeth and Anna's sorrow by sharing with them their own deep love for the Catholic faith. Elizabeth returned home to New York convinced that she would become a Catholic. Her family and friends didn't understand and were upset with her decision. But Elizabeth went ahead with courage. She joined the Catholic Church on March 14, 1805.

A few years later, Elizabeth was asked to come and open a girls' school in Baltimore. It was there that Elizabeth decided to live as a religious sister. Many women came to join her, including her sister and sister-in-law. Her own daughters, Anna and Catherine, also joined the group. They became the Sisters of Charity, and Elizabeth was given the title "Mother Seton." The sisters' first house was small, with no running water. In the winter, they would wake up in the morning covered with a dusting of snow that had fallen through the roof! They had to walk several miles every Sunday to attend Mass in town.

More young women came to join Mother Seton, and the community grew. The sisters moved into a larger house, and Elizabeth's good works continued to spread. Besides founding many Catholic schools, she also opened orphanages. She even made plans for a hospital, which was begun after her death. Elizabeth loved to write. She also translated some textbooks from French to English. But she was best known for the way she visited the poor and the sick.

Elizabeth was canonized a saint by Pope Paul VI on September 14, 1975. She is the first U.S.-born citizen to be declared a saint.

Whenever we have a problem we can talk to God about it. He will always help us to know what to do. When we trust God as St. Elizabeth Seton did, he will bring good out of even difficult situations.

January 5

St. John Neumann

John Nepomucene Neumann was born on March 28, 1811, in Bohemia, which is now part of the Czech Republic. His parents were Philip and Agnes Neumann. John had four sisters and a brother. After finishing college, he entered the seminary. John was very intelligent and did really well in his studies. He learned to speak eight modern languages fluently, besides Latin, Greek, and Hebrew!

But when it came time for ordination, there was a problem. John could not be ordained because Bohemia had more than enough priests just then! Since he had been reading about missionary activities in the United States, John decided to go to America to be ordained. He walked most of the way to France and then boarded the ship *Europa*.

John arrived in Manhattan on June 9, 1836. Bishop John Dubois was very happy to see him. There were only thirty-six priests to serve the 200,000 Catholics living in the state of New York and part of New Jersey. Just sixteen days after his arrival, John was ordained a priest and sent to Buffalo, New York. There he would help Father Pax care for his parish, which was 900 square miles in size. "Father John, would you like to work in the city or in a country area?" Father Pax asked him. Now John's heroic character began to show. "I'd like to work in the country," John responded. He knew that this was the more difficult area. Father John decided to stay in a little town with an unfinished church. Once it was completed, he moved to another town that had a log-church. There he built himself a small log cabin. The farms in his area were far apart. John had to walk long distances to reach his people. They were German, French, Irish and Scotch. In addition to the languages he already spoke, John now learned English and Gaelic. Before he died, he knew and spoke twelve different languages!

Father John joined the Redemptorist Order and continued his missionary work. He became bishop of Philadelphia in 1852. Bishop John Neumann built fifty churches and began building a cathedral. He opened almost one hundred schools. During the time he was bishop, the number of parochial school students grew from 500 to 9,000. Bishop John made sure to visit all his parishes on a regular basis. Once, he even walked twenty-five miles both ways to administer the sacrament of Confirmation to a boy.

Bishop John died suddenly on January 5, 1860. He was walking home from an appointment when he suffered a stroke and fell to the ground. He was carried into the nearest house and died there at 3:00 P.M. Bishop John Neumann would have been forty-nine that March. He was proclaimed a saint by Pope Paul VI on June 19, 1977.

St. John put his whole self into the work God gave him to do. Instead of looking for an easier life, he chose to do as much as he could and as cheerfully as possible. The little everyday things we must do are the work God gives us. Like St. John Neumann, let's do them with all our hearts.

January 6

St. André Bessette

Alfred Bessette was born on August 9, 1845, not far from Montreal, Canada. He was the eighth of twelve children. When Alfred was nine, his father, a woodcutter, died in an accident at work. Three years later, Alfred's mother died of tuberculosis. The Bessette children were placed in different homes. Alfred went to live with his aunt and uncle.

Because his family had been so poor and he was often sick, Alfred had very little education. So for the next thirteen years he tried learning farming, shoemaking and baking. He even worked in a factory in Connecticut. But his poor health kept him from continuing a trade.

When Alfred was twenty-five years old, he joined the Congregation of the Holy Cross and chose the name Brother André. He spent the next forty years as a general maintenance man and messenger. The remaining years of his life were spent as the doorkeeper for his congregation's college. Here, Brother André became known for his healing power. When people came to ask him for a cure, he would tell them to first thank God for their suffering because it was so valuable. Then he would pray with them. Most of the people he prayed with were cured. Brother André always refused credit for any healing. He insisted that cures were due to the person's faith in God and the intercession of St. Joseph.

Brother André had a great love for the Eucharist and for St. Joseph. When he was young, he dreamt he saw a big church, but he couldn't tell where it was. Little by little he came to realize that God wanted a church built in honor of St. Joseph. That church was to be erected on top of Mount Royale in Montreal, Canada. Prayer and the sacrifices of Brother André and many other people made the dream come true. The magnificent church honoring St. Joseph was built. It is called St. Joseph's Oratory and is a testimony to Brother André's great faith. Pilgrims continue to come to St. Joseph's all year long. Some come from distant places. They want to honor St. Joseph and show their trust in his loving care, as Brother André did.

Brother André died peacefully on January 6, 1937. Nearly a million people climbed Mount Royale to St. Joseph's Oratory for his funeral. They came in spite of sleet and snow to say good-bye to their dear friend. Brother André was proclaimed "blessed" on May 23, 1982, by Pope John Paul II. Pope Benedict XVI canonized André on October 17, 2010.

Brother André is remembered for his deep devotion to St. Joseph, which helped him to live a holy life. We can learn a lot from the examples of the saints. By reading about their lives and praying to them, we will form close friendships with them. The saints will help us to live as good friends of Jesus— just as they did.

January 7

St. Raymond of Peñafort

Raymond was born in 1175 in a little town near Barcelona, Spain. He was educated at the cathedral school in Barcelona and became a priest. Raymond graduated from law school in Bologna, Italy, and became a famous teacher. He joined the Dominican Order in 1222 and became a priest. Father Raymond preached throughout Spain, hearing confessions and bringing many people back to God and the Church.

In 1230, Pope Gregory IX asked him to come to Rome. When Raymond arrived, the Pope gave him several assignments. One duty was to collect and publish all the official letters of the popes since 1150, which was the last time such a work had been done. It took Raymond three years to gather all the letters. He published them in five books. Raymond also helped to write Church law.

In 1238, Raymond was elected master general (the highest superior) of the Dominicans. With his knowledge of law, he revised the order's rule, making it clearer and easier to understand. At the age of sixty-five, he resigned his position and dedicated the rest of his life to parish work. That is what he *really* wanted to do. His compassion helped many people return to God through the sacrament of Reconciliation.

During his years in Rome, Raymond learned of the difficulties that missionaries were having. They were trying hard to bring the Gospel to people in Northern Africa and Spain. To help the missionaries, Raymond started a school that taught the language and culture of the people to be evangelized. Father Raymond also asked the famous Dominican, St. Thomas Aquinas, to write a booklet. This booklet would explain the truths of the Catholic faith in a way that non-Christians could understand. (We celebrate the feast of St. Thomas on January 28.)

Raymond lived nearly one hundred years. He died in Barcelona on January 6, 1275. He was proclaimed a saint in 1601 by Pope Clement VIII. This pope declared Raymond the patron of Church lawyers because of his great influence on Church law.

St. Raymond could never have done as much as he did without his love for prayer and for the Blessed Mother. Sometimes, when we have a lot to do, we might think that we're too busy to pray. But when we put God first and make time for prayer, God will always help us, and we'll be surprised to see how much we get done!

January 8

St. Andrew Corsini

Andrew Corsini was born in Italy in 1302. Before he was born, his mother had a mysterious dream. She dreamt that she gave birth to a wolf. In her dream, the wolf went into a church and was changed into a lamb. Later, when Andrew was living an out-of-control life as a young man, his mother told him, "You are the wolf I dreamt about." The next day, Andrew went into a Carmelite church to pray. While he was praying, he felt inspired to change his life and become a Carmelite priest.

As a priest, Andrew worked in Florence, and then went to France to continue his studies. He became well known for his gifts of prophecy and healing. He also was able to convince sinners to repent and lead holy lives. Once he even helped his cousin overcome a gambling problem.

In 1349, Andrew was chosen to be bishop of Fiesole. Because he felt he was not worthy, Andrew tried to hide. But a child found him by accident, and he was made a bishop. He lived a humble life and practiced penances. Every Thursday he washed the feet of the poor in memory of the time that Jesus washed his apostles' feet on Holy Thursday. Besides his works of kindness to the poor, Bishop Andrew also became known as a peacemaker, and he was sent by the pope to Bologna to settle a dispute between the nobility and the people of that city.

Bishop Andrew Corsini became ill on Christmas night in 1372, and died on January 6, 1373. He was declared a saint in 1629.

We can be peacemakers just like St. Andrew. When we treat people with love and respect, we are spreading peace. When we forgive those who have hurt us, we are spreading peace. When we try to cheer up people who are sad, we are spreading peace.

January 9

St. Adrian of Canterbury

Adrian was from Africa. He became a Benedictine monk in a monastery near Naples, Italy. He would have preferred to remain a simple monk, but his holiness and intelligence led his community to choose him as their abbot.

After a few years, the archbishop of Canterbury, England died. Pope Vitalian chose Adrian to take his place. But Adrian didn't want a position of such importance. He asked the pope to choose someone else. Adrian even recommended Theodore of Tarsus, who was also well qualified. The pope agreed, but he asked Adrian to go to Canterbury with Theodore, as his adviser.

On the way to England, Theodore and Adrian were arrested in France. They were suspected of being supporters of the Byzantine emperor who wanted to take over the west. They were kept in custody for two years. After their release, they finally made their way to England, where Theodore took his place as archbishop of Canterbury. Theodore named Adrian abbot of Saints Peter and Paul Monastery, which later became St. Augustine's. Adrian was abbot of this monastery for thirty-nine years. He turned it into a wonderful center of learning. Adrian taught Sacred Scripture, theology, law, Greek, and Latin at the monastery.

Adrian died in the year 710 on January 9. He was buried in his monastery, which quickly became famous for the miracles that took place there.

St. Adrian would have chosen to live the quiet life of a monk. But God had other plans. He wanted

Adrian to travel and to be very active. This shows
that we can be close to God no matter what we are
doing or where we are. We are always close to God
because God lives in our hearts.

January 10

St. John the Almsgiver

John was a dedicated Christian nobleman from
the island of Cyprus. He used his wealth and position
to help poor people. After his wife and child died,
John gave his belongings to the poor and became a
priest. Later he was ordained a bishop. In 608, Bishop
John was consecrated the patriarch of Alexandria,
Egypt. What could people expect of this man who
now had such an important position? John focused
his efforts on healing the divisions among his people.
He made up his mind to practice a "charity without
limits." The first thing he did was to ask for a complete
list of his "masters." "What do you mean?" the other
priests asked in surprise. "I mean that I would like a
list of all the poor people in Alexandria," Bishop John
explained. "They will be my masters because I have
come to serve them." Bishop John discovered that
there were 7,500 poor people living in Alexandria! He
promised to be their personal protector.

As patriarch, Bishop John passed laws and corrected things that were not right. He was respectful

and kind, but firm. Every Wednesday and Friday he met with anyone who wished to see him. People lined up and waited patiently for their turn. Some were rich. Some were homeless and destitute. All received the same respect and attention. When John found out that the church treasury had 80,000 pieces of gold, he divided it all among the hospitals and monasteries. He set up a system that provided poor people with the money they needed to support themselves. He warmly welcomed refugees from neighboring areas. After the Persians had plundered Jerusalem, Bishop John sent money and supplies to the suffering people. He even sent workmen to assist in rebuilding the churches there.

When people wanted to know how Bishop John could be so charitable and unselfish, he had an amazing answer. Once when he was very young he had a dream or vision. He saw a beautiful girl and he realized that she represented "charity." She told him: "I am the oldest daughter of the King. If you are devoted to me, I will lead you to Jesus. No one is as powerful with him as I am. Remember, it was for me that he became a baby to redeem humankind." John never tired of telling about that vision. He gently led the rich to be generous. He helped the poor trust that God would always be there for them.

St. John died peacefully on November 11, 619. Because of his great charity, he is called "the almsgiver," which means someone who gives money, food, or clothing to those who need it.

Sometimes we might be tempted to think only of ourselves. When we have thoughts and attitudes like this, we can pray to St. John. We can ask him to teach us to be as loving and generous as he was.

January 11

St. Bernard of Corleone

Philip Latini was born in 1605. When he grew up, he became a shoemaker in Sicily, Italy. Philip did not lead a very religious life. In fact, he hardly ever thought about God. Once in a while he even found himself in trouble with the law.

Philip was a skilled swordsman. One day in 1632, he wounded a police officer. He ran into a church so that he couldn't be arrested. While he was there, he had time to think. Little by little, a change began to come over him. Philip realized that if he continued living his life as he was, he would spend the rest of it in jail! God gave him the grace to want to live a better life.

Philip entered the Capuchin Order as a lay brother. He received the new name Bernard. He devoted himself to prayer, penance, and humble service. He spent the second half of his life making up for the sins he had committed in the first half.

God was pleased with Bernard, and even blessed him with many special gifts. Bernard soon became known for his miracles and prophecies. He also had the gift of levitation, which means that he would sometimes rise off the ground while he was praying. Bernard died on January 12, 1667 in Palermo, Italy. He was canonized in 2001 by Pope John Paul II.

To become saints, we don't have to be able to perform miracles as St. Bernard did. These gifts are not what made the saints holy. Loving God and other people, praying and obeying the Ten Commandments are what make a person holy. These are the things we should try to imitate in the lives of the saints.

January 12

St. Marguerite Bourgeoys

Marguerite was born in Troyes, France, on April 17, 1620. She was the sixth of twelve children. Her parents were hardworking, religious people. When Marguerite was nineteen, her mother died. Marguerite took care of her younger brothers and sisters. Her father died when she was twenty-seven. The family was now raised, and Marguerite prayed to know what to do with her life. The governor of Montreal, Canada, was visiting France at that time, trying to find teachers for the New World. He invited Marguerite to come to Montreal to teach school and religion classes. She accepted.

Marguerite gave the inheritance her parents had left to her to other members of the family. They couldn't believe that she would really leave their civilized country to go to live in the wilderness an ocean away. But on June 20, 1653, she did just that. She sailed from France and arrived in Canada in mid-November. Marguerite began the construction of a chapel in honor of Our Lady of Good Help in 1657. She opened her first school in 1658. Soon Marguerite realized that she needed more teachers. She sailed to France in 1659 and returned to Canada with four companions. In 1670, she went to France again. This time she brought six more teachers back to Canada with her. These brave women became the first sisters of the Congregation of Notre Dame.

Mother Marguerite and her sisters helped people in the colony survive when food was scarce. They opened a vocational school and taught young people how to run a home and farm. Mother Marguerite's congregation was growing. By 1681 there were eighteen sisters. Seven of them were Canadian. They opened more missions, including a Native American mission. Mother Marguerite herself received the first two Native American women into the congregation.

In 1693, Mother Marguerite asked Sr. Marie Barbier, the first Canadian to join the order, to take over as the community's superior. The Church approved Marguerite's religious rule in 1698. Marguerite spent her last few years praying and writing the story of her life. On the last day of 1699, a young sister lay dying.

Mother Marguerite asked the Lord to take her own life in exchange. By the morning of January 1, 1700, the sister was completely well, and Mother Marguerite had a very high fever. She suffered for twelve days and died on January 12, 1700. Pope John Paul II proclaimed Marguerite Bourgeoys a saint on April 2, 1982.

When we feel we don't have enough courage to do what God asks of us, we can ask St. Marguerite to make us brave and generous like her. We can ask her to help us to be more concerned about others than about our personal comfort.

January 13

St. Hilary of Poitiers

In the early centuries of Christianity, there were still many people who did not believe in God as we do. They believed that there were many gods, some more powerful than others. In the year 315, Hilary was born into just such a family in Poitiers, a town in France. His family was rich and well known. Hilary received a good education. He married and raised a family.

Through his studies, Hilary learned that a person should practice patience, kindness, justice and as many good habits as possible. These good acts would be rewarded in the life after death. Hilary's studies also convinced him that there could only be *one* God who is eternal, all-powerful and good. He read the Bible for the first time. When he came to the story of Moses and the burning bush, Hilary was very impressed by the name God gave himself: I AM WHO AM. Hilary read the writings of the prophets, too. Then he read the whole New Testament. By the time he finished, Hilary was completely converted to Christianity, and he asked to be baptized.

Hilary lived the faith so well that he was appointed a bishop. This did not make his life easy because the emperor was interfering in Church matters. When Hilary opposed him, the emperor exiled him. That was when Hilary's great virtues of patience and courage stood out. He accepted exile calmly and used the time to write books explaining the Catholic faith.

Since he was becoming famous, Hilary's enemies asked the emperor to send him back to his home in France. They hoped that people would pay less attention to him there. So Hilary was sent back to Poitiers in 360. He continued writing and teaching the people about the faith. Hilary died eight years later, at the age of fifty-two. His books have influenced the Church right to our own day. That is why he is called a Doctor of the Church.

Faith is a wonderful gift from God. Because St. Hilary was honest in seeking the truth, God blessed him with the gift of faith. We have received the gift of faith too. Let's try to make our faith stronger by praying every day and by always being eager to learn more about God.

January 14

St. Macrina the Elder

On January 2, we celebrated the feast of St. Basil the Great, who was a grandchild of today's saint, St. Macrina. Basil, who was born around 329, came from a family of saints. Macrina, his father's mother, was one of his favorites. She seems to have raised Basil. As an adult, Basil praised his grandmother for all the good she had done for him. He especially thanked her for having taught him to love the Christian faith from the time he was very small.

Macrina and her husband learned the high price of being true to their Christian beliefs. During one of the Roman persecutions, they were forced into hiding. They found refuge in the forest near their home. Somehow the couple managed to escape their persecutors. They were always hungry and afraid, but they would not give up their faith. Instead, they patiently waited and prayed for the terrible persecution to end. It lasted for seven long years. During that time Macrina and her husband hunted for food. They managed to survive by eating wild vegetation. St. Gregory Nazianzen, who shares St. Basil's feast day on January 2, is the one who wrote down these few details about St. Basil's grandparents.

During another persecution, Macrina and her husband had all their property and belongings taken from them. They were left with nothing but their faith and trust in God's care for them.

St. Macrina lived longer than her husband, but the exact year of each of their deaths is not known. It is believed that Macrina died around 340. Her grandchild, St. Basil, died in 379.

St. Macrina was a loving grandmother. She showed Basil and the rest of her family the beauty of Christianity by really living all that she believed in. We can ask St. Macrina to help us to be strong Christians too.

January 15

St. Paul the Hermit

Paul was born into a Christian family in the year 229. They lived in Thebes, Egypt. Paul's parents showed him by their own lives how to love God and worship him with one's whole heart. Paul was very sad to lose both his parents when he was just fifteen years old.

A few years later, in 250, Emperor Decius started a cruel persecution of the Christians. Paul hid in his friend's home, but he still wasn't safe. His brother-in-law was after his money and property. Paul realized that this greedy relative could easily betray him to the authorities, so he ran away to the desert. Paul found a cave near a palm tree and a spring of fresh water and he settled there. He sewed palm branches together for clothes, and he lived on fruit and water.

Paul had intended to stay in the desert only until the persecution was over. But by the time it ended, he had fallen in love with his life of prayer. He felt so close to God. How could he give it all up? He decided to remain in the desert and never return to his wealthy city life. He would spend his life praying for the needs of all people and offering God penances to make up for sin.

There was another holy hermit living in the desert at that same time. His name was Anthony. Anthony thought he was the only hermit. But God showed Paul to him in a dream and told Anthony to go visit him.

Paul was so happy to see Anthony because he knew he was going to die in a few days. Anthony was sad because he didn't want to lose his new friend so soon. But, as Paul predicted, he died on January 15, 342, at the age of 113. Anthony buried him in a cloak that had belonged to St. Athanasius. Then Anthony took home the garment of palm leaves that Paul had been wearing. He never forgot his wonderful friend.

We should feel a close connection with those who are in heaven. We can treasure a keepsake, or even a beautiful memory, of someone we love who has died, just as St. Anthony treasured the garment of St. Paul. This way we feel them close to us until we meet them again in heaven.

January 16

St. Berard and Companions

Five Franciscan friars accepted from St. Francis of Assisi an assignment to preach the Gospel in Morocco. Friars Berard, Peter, Adjutus, Accursio and Odo traveled by ship in 1219. Morocco is in the northwest corner of Africa, and the journey was long and dangerous. The group first arrived at Seville, Spain. They started preaching immediately, in streets and in public squares. People treated them as if they were crazy and had them arrested. To save themselves from being sent back home, the friars explained that they were on their way to see the sultan in Morocco. So the governor of Seville sent them to Morocco.

The sultan received the friars and gave them freedom to preach in the city. But some of the people didn't like this. They complained to the authorities. The sultan tried to save the friars by sending them to live in Marrakech, on the west coast of Morocco. A Christian prince and friend of the sultan, Dom Pedro Fernandez, took them into his home. But the friars knew that their mission was to preach the Catholic faith. They returned to the city as often as they could. This angered some people who didn't want to hear the friars' message. These complaints annoyed the sultan so much that one day when he saw the friars preaching, he ordered them to stop or leave the country. Since they didn't feel it was right for them to do either one, they were beheaded right then and there. It was January 16, 1220.

Dom Pedro went to claim the bodies of the martyrs. Eventually he brought their relics to Holy Cross Church in Coimbra, Portugal. The friars' mission to Morocco had been brief and an apparent failure. But the results were surprising. The story of these heroes fired the first Franciscans with the desire to be missionaries and martyrs, too. It was the particular witness of Berard and his companions that inspired a young man to dedicate his life to God as a Franciscan priest. We know him as St. Anthony of Padua, whose feast day is June 13.

As long as we try our best, we don't have to worry about the success or failure of what we do. St. Berard and his companions seemed to fail in their preaching mission, but their love for Jesus inspired other people. God can always use our effort and dedication to help people live better lives.

January 17

St. Anthony of Egypt

St. Anthony was born in 251 in a small village in Egypt. When he was twenty years old, his parents died. They left him a large estate and placed him in charge of the care of his younger sister. Anthony felt overwhelmed and turned to God in prayer. Gradually he became more and more aware of the power of God in his life. About six months later, he heard this quotation of Jesus from the Gospel: "Go, sell what you own and give the money to the poor, and you will have treasure in heaven" (Mark 10:21). He took the words as a personal message in answer to his prayer for guidance. Anthony sold most of his possessions, keeping only enough to support his sister and himself. Then he gave the rest of the money to people who needed it.

Anthony's sister joined a group of women living a life of prayer and contemplation. Anthony decided to become a hermit. He begged an elderly hermit to teach him about the spiritual life. Anthony also visited other hermits so that he could learn each one's most outstanding virtue. Then he began his own life of prayer and penance alone with God.

When he was fifty-five, Anthony built a monastery where monks could worship and serve God together. Many people heard of his holiness and came to him for advice. Anthony would tell them how they could become closer to God. Once he said, "The devil is afraid of us when we pray and make sacrifices and when we are humble and good. He is especially afraid when we love Jesus very much. He runs away when we make the Sign of the Cross."

St. Anthony visited Paul the hermit (whose feast is celebrated on January 15). He learned a lot from the example of Paul's holy life. Anthony died after a long, prayerful life. He was 105 years old. St. Athanasius wrote a well-known biography of St. Anthony of Egypt. (St. Athanasius's feast day is May 2.)

God was first in St. Anthony's life. Sometimes we can think we need everything we see advertised on TV to make us happy. But no amount of money or things can make us really happy. Only loving and serving God can.

January 18

Blessed Christina Ciccarelli

Blessed Christina lived in the sixteenth century. She was born in Abruzzi, Italy. Her baptismal name was Matthia. As she grew up, Matthia felt God calling her to a life of prayer and penance. She chose to become a cloistered nun. Matthia entered the convent of St. Augustine in Aquila. She was called Sister Christina.

Sister Christina's life as a nun was hidden and silent. But the people of Aquila soon realized that she and the other nuns were bringing many blessings to them through their prayer and loving dedication. Even though Sister Christina never left her convent, she was very aware of the needs of the poor people of her area. She and the nuns provided whatever they could for them. Sister Christina also paid attention to the sufferings of others. She prayed and offered sacrifices for all those who suffered.

Jesus sometimes gave Sister Christina the ability to know the future. The Lord even used her to work miracles for the good of others. When she died on January 18, 1543, a large crowd of people came to honor and thank her for the gift she had been for their city.

There are many different ways to help others. Blessed Christina shows us how to help other people by praying for them and being attentive to their needs and sufferings.

January 19

St. Paula

Paula was born in 347 in Rome. She belonged to a wealthy, noble family. When she grew up, she married a man named Toxotius. They lived a happy married life and had five children.

When Paula was thirty-two years old, her husband died. Paula began to live a life completely dedicated to God. She devoted herself to prayer and to reading the Bible. She offered God the sacrifice of her fasting. Because she was wealthy, she was able to help the poor and needy.

Paula was fortunate to have the holy and learned priest, St. Jerome, to give her good advice. (We celebrate the feast of St. Jerome on September 30.) From him, Paula learned the importance of reading and studying Holy Scripture. When Paula's oldest daughter died, Jerome comforted her in her time of sorrow. He helped her to rely on her faith in God and the hope of heaven.

When St. Jerome made a journey to the Holy Land to work on his translation of the Bible into Latin, Paula went with him. There she saw the places where Jesus lived and taught. She decided to live in Bethlehem, and she established a convent there, where she lived a simple life of prayer. She helped St. Jerome in his work, and he valued her knowledge of the Bible. Paula continued to use her money to build churches and monasteries in the Holy Land. She also took care of St. Jerome.

Paula died on January 26, in 404. She had lived in Bethlehem for twenty years. She was buried beneath the Church of the Nativity. She is the patron saint of widows.

St. Paula was able to bear suffering and loss in her life because of her faith and trust in God. She knew God very well because she read his Word daily. An important part of being close to God is allowing him to speak to us in Sacred Scripture. It's good to set aside a little time each day to read the Bible and make it part of our lives.

January 20

St. Fabian and St. Sebastian

Fabian, who lived in Rome, was the first man who was not a priest to be elected pope. He was elected pope in the year 236. We know very little about this saint. It is said that he was chosen to be pope because a dove rested on his head during the election. We do know that Fabian spoke out against Bishop Privatus who was spreading false teachings in Africa. Pope Fabian was also responsible for having the catacombs (underground Roman cemeteries where many of the early Christians were buried) repaired and restored. In the year 250, he died a martyr's death during Emperor Decius' persecution. St. Fabian is buried in the Basilica of St. Sebastian. The two martyrs share the same feast day.

Sebastian was a soldier in the Roman army from 283 to 288. According to legend, he gave encouragement to the Christians who were condemned to death for their faith. He also convinced many pagans to embrace Christianity. Emperor Diocletian didn't know that Sebastian was a Christian, and he made him captain of the praetorian guards (men who guarded a Roman commander or emperor). When Maximian became emperor, he discovered that Sebastian was a Christian and ordered him to be put to death. Sebastian was shot with arrows.

When the Christians came to bury him, they realized he was still alive! They cared for him until he got well again. Soon after this, Sebastian confronted the emperor and spoke out against his cruel treatment of the Christians. The emperor, shocked to see him alive, ordered that Sebastian be beaten to death. St. Sebastian is the patron saint of archers, athletes, and soldiers.

St. Fabian and St. Sebastian were very different from one another. One was a pope and the other was a soldier. They teach us that Jesus loves us individually, just as we are. Like Fabian and Sebastian, we each have our own gift to give others. The important thing is to give our gifts with all our hearts.

January 21

St. Agnes

Much of Agnes' story comes down to us in the form of legend, but it is a fact that she was a martyr in the early fourth century. She has always been a popular saint because St. Ambrose and other well-known early Church saints have written about her.

Agnes was a beautiful young girl who belonged to a wealthy Roman family. She loved God very

much and wanted to give her heart only to him. She chose Jesus as her spouse and would not marry anyone else.

Because Agnes was rich and beautiful, many young Roman noblemen wanted to marry her. But she answered them all by saying, "I already have a husband in heaven—Jesus." The young men became angry and reported Agnes to the governor, accusing her of being a Christian. This was in the year 304, when Christians were being put to death by order of the emperor Diocletian.

Even though Agnes was only thirteen years old, she faced the governor bravely. She would not turn away from God. She would not burn incense to the idols. She wasn't even afraid when the governor threatened to have her tortured. This made the governor so angry that he sent Agnes to the house of some evil women, so that they could lead her to sin. But Agnes remained pure and holy, trusting in Jesus, who made her strong.

When Agnes was brought back to the governor, he ordered her to be beheaded. Agnes bowed her head before the executioner. She felt happy to give her life for Jesus, and she looked forward to being with him soon in heaven. In one stroke, the executioner cut off Agnes' head. She is buried in a cemetery named after her. In 354, Emperor Constantine's daughter built a large church there and had Agnes' body placed under the altar. St. Agnes' symbol is the lamb.

St. Agnes made heroic decisions and stuck to them. She could do this because she made Jesus the center of her life. Her love for Jesus gave her the strength she needed to be true to her Christian faith. We can ask St. Agnes for her courage and love for Jesus.

January 22

St. Vincent of Saragossa

St. Vincent was born in Huesca, in Spain. He was educated by Valerius, the bishop of Huesca. Bishop Valerius ordained Vincent a deacon and gave him the task of preaching, even though he was still young. This was because Bishop Valerius recognized Vincent's talents and goodness.

In 304, both Vincent and Bishop Valerius were arrested by Dacian, the governor of Spain. The emperors Diocletian and Maximian had published a decree ordering that all Christians be put to death. Vincent and Valerius were imprisoned in Valencia, where they suffered from hunger and were treated cruelly. When they were brought before Dacian, Vincent spoke for both of them, saying they were ready to suffer and die for the true God.

Dacian banished Valerius from Spain. But he handed Vincent over to be tortured. In spite of the terrible pains he suffered, Vincent remained peaceful and strong in his faith. He refused to sacrifice to idols or to hand over the sacred books of his church to be burned. The more pains he endured, the more strength God gave him.

When the tortures were over, Vincent was brought back to his prison cell. No one was allowed to bring him food or visit him. When the prison warden saw Vincent's faith and his peaceful attitude, he was convinced that Vincent worshiped the true God, and he became a Christian. After this, Emperor Dacian allowed Vincent to have visitors. The Christians came to his dungeon to take care of him, but a short time later Vincent died.

St. Vincent remained strong during a time of persecution because of the influence of the holy bishop, Valerius. Vincent had learned from the bishop what it takes to be a follower of Jesus. Let's ask St. Vincent to help us recognize and follow the good example of others.

January 23

St. Marianne Cope

Maria Anna Barbara Koob was born on January 23, 1838, to a poor farming family in Germany. About a year later they moved to America and settled in Utica, New York. Her father changed the family name to Cope. He later became sick and was unable to work. So Barbara got a job in a factory to help support the family. In her heart she had a strong desire to serve God. When the other children were older and the family did not need her help, she entered the Sisters of St. Francis in Syracuse in 1862.

She became known as Sister Marianne and was soon teaching. She had many talents and she helped to establish two new Catholic hospitals. She was put in charge of St. Joseph's hospital. She took care of many patients and ran the hospital efficiently. Later she became the superior of her community.

In 1883, the king of Hawaii wrote asking for help to take care of people with leprosy. So Mother Marianne went to Hawaii with some other sisters. Once there, she started Malulani Hospital in Maui, and a few years later she began a home for girls. In November 1888, Mother Marianne went to Kalaupapa on the island of Molokai. Her mission was to care for women and girls who had leprosy. There, she met Father Damien, who had spent his life caring for the lepers. He was ill and died a few months later.

For the next thirty years, Mother Marianne totally dedicated herself to caring for the people on Molokai. She died on August 9, 1918, and was canonized on October 21, 2012.

Mother Marianne always saw Jesus in everyone she met. She once said, "I do not think of reward; I am working for God, and do so cheerfully." Her life teaches us how to be willing to help others and serve them in their needs.

January 24

St. Francis de Sales

Francis de Sales was born in his family's castle at Savoy, France, on August 21, 1567. Because he was born two months early, he was very weak as a baby. But he grew strong and healthy and was a very obedient and kind little boy.

Francis's mother taught him to pray. She read the lives of the saints to him, and took him with her whenever she went out to visit the poor. He received a very good education. He studied at Annecy, and then went to Paris to attend the Jesuit College of Clermont. After this he went on to study law and theology at the University of Padua. By the age of twenty-four, Francis had already earned a doctorate in law.

Francis's world was opening up to him with many promises of a successful career. But he felt called to the priesthood. It was hard to persuade his disappointed father, but Francis followed God's call and became a priest on December 18, 1593.

He volunteered to go to Chablais to work as a missionary among many people who had left the Church and were very unfriendly toward priests. Even though some of these people tried to kill him, Father Francis continued working among them. His patience and kindness brought many back to the Church.

In 1602, Francis was made bishop of Geneva, Switzerland. He worked very hard to bring unity back to the Church at a time when there were many problems. He opened schools, taught and preached.

In 1604, Francis met a holy woman named Jane Frances de Chantal. (Jane later became a saint too.) He became her spiritual director, and in 1610 he helped her found the Order of the Visitation, a new order of sisters.

Francis de Sales wrote many wonderful books about God and the way to become closer to him. In these books Francis taught that holiness is possible in everyday life, and that God calls us all to become saints. Some of Francis's books, like *Introduction to the Devout Life,* written in 1609, and *Treatise on the Love of God,* written in 1616, are still in print today.

Bishop Francis de Sales died in Lyons, France, on December 28, 1622. He was fifty-six years old. Pope Innocent X declared Francis a saint in 1665. Because of his heroic dedication to the Church, he was given the special title "Doctor of the Church." He is also the patron saint of journalists.

We can learn many lessons from St. Francis de Sales. He shows us that with love and patience, we can bring many people closer to Jesus. The best way to preach the Gospel of Jesus is to live it sincerely.

Conversion of St. Paul

Saul was a Jew, born in Tarsus and brought up in Jerusalem. As a young man, he was very zealous for the Jewish law and traditions. He thought that the Christian way of life was something opposed to God and his law. Because of this, Saul persecuted the Christians with all his might.

One day, Saul headed for Damascus with some men. He had permission to capture any Christians he could find in the city and bring them back to Jerusalem to be imprisoned and punished. Just before he got to the city, a bright light flashed around him and he fell to the ground. A voice called to him, "Saul! Saul! Why are you persecuting me?"

Saul was confused. He asked the voice, "Who are you, Sir?"

The voice answered, "I am Jesus, the one you are persecuting."

"What do you want me to do?" Saul asked.

Jesus told Saul to go to Damascus, where he would find out what he should do. At that moment, through the power of God, Saul received the gift to believe in Jesus. Weak and trembling, he reached out for help. His companions led him into Damascus. Now that he was blind he could really "see" the truth. And Jesus had come personally to meet him, to invite

him to conversion. In Damascus, a Christian named Ananias stood before him and said, "Brother Saul, receive your sight back." And Saul could see again!

Ananias told Saul that God had chosen him to tell many people in many lands about Jesus. Saul was baptized, and started to live the life of a Christian. He used his Roman name, Paul, from then on because he had been chosen by God to go to the people who were not Jewish and tell them about Jesus.

St. Paul traveled all over the world, preaching the Good News. He led countless people to Jesus. He worked and suffered. His enemies tried to kill him several times, but nothing could stop him. When Paul was old and tired, he was once again put in prison and sentenced to die. Still St. Paul was happy to suffer and even die for Christ.

This great apostle wrote wonderful letters to the Christians. They are in the Bible. These letters, called epistles, are read often during the Liturgy of the Word at Mass.

The story of St. Paul's conversion is found in the Acts of the Apostles, in chapters 9, 22, and 26. For more about St. Paul, see June 29, the Feast of St. Peter and St. Paul.

St. Paul's conversion was very important for the life of the Church. But Jesus calls us just as he called Paul on the road to Damascus. He invites us to give up doing whatever keeps us from coming closer to him. Let's ask St. Paul to help us.

January 26

St. Timothy and St. Titus

Besides having been bishops in the early Church, Timothy and Titus have something else in common. Both men received the gift of faith through the preaching of St. Paul.

Timothy was born at Lystra, in Asia Minor. His father was Greek and his mother was Jewish. When Paul came to preach in Lystra, Timothy, his mother and his grandmother all became Christians. Several years later, Paul went back to Lystra. Timothy was grown up now, and Paul felt that God was calling him to be a missionary. Paul invited Timothy to join him in preaching the Gospel. And so Timothy left his home and parents to follow Paul. Paul and Timothy shared both the joys and sufferings of bringing the Word of God to many, many people. Timothy was like a son to Paul. He went everywhere with him until he became bishop of Ephesus. Then Timothy stayed at Ephesus to shepherd his people. St. Timothy died a martyr, just as St. Paul had.

Titus was a Gentile (a non-Jewish person) converted by St. Paul. He became Paul's secretary and was with him at the Council of Jerusalem. Titus was generous and hardworking. He joyfully preached the Good News with Paul on their missionary travels. Because Titus was so trustworthy, Paul freely sent him on many "missions" to the Christian communities. Titus helped people strengthen their faith in Jesus. He had a special gift for being a peacemaker and was able to bring Christians together again after there had been arguments among them. Paul appreciated this gift in Titus and recognized it as the Holy Spirit's work.

While preaching in Crete, Paul was called away to other churches that needed him. Not wanting to leave the Christians at Crete without a shepherd, he ordained Titus bishop and left him there to continue his work. Titus remained at Crete for the rest of his life. Paul wrote a letter to him from Macedonia in the year 65.

St. Timothy and St. Titus gave their whole lives—their time and energy—to Jesus. They were true disciples of St. Paul. It's easy to overlook the people in our lives who help us better understand our faith. Let's pray today for all who spread the Good News as Paul, Timothy, and Titus did.

January 27

St. Angela Merici

Angela Merici was born on March 21, 1470, at Desenzano, Lombardy, in Northern Italy. She was orphaned at age ten, and she and her sister went to live with their uncle at Salo, a nearby town.

When she was thirteen years old, Angela joined the Secular Franciscan Order (also called the Third Order), and began to live a life of prayer and self-discipline.

In 1495 her uncle died, and Angela moved back to Desenzano. Here she had a vision. She saw herself teaching a group of young girls. Angela invited some of her Third Order friends to help her teach girls from poor families, and she opened a school in her home. In 1516, she was asked to come to Brescia to start another school just like it.

Angela made a pilgrimage to the Holy Land. During the trip, she lost her sight, but miraculously received it back. In 1525 Angela went to Rome for the Holy Year. While she was there, Pope Clement VII asked her if she would like to be the superior of a community of nursing sisters. But she explained that God wanted her to devote herself to teaching the poor, and she went back to Brescia.

In 1533 Angela started training a group of women to be teachers. By November 25, 1535, there were twenty-eight women in the group. Together with Angela they wanted to dedicate their lives to God and to teaching young girls, especially the poor. They chose St. Ursula, the patroness of medieval universities, as their patron saint. The women remained in their own homes at first. Because of many difficulties, it was a long time before they could live together in a convent. But little by little this community of young women started by St. Angela developed into the Ursuline Sisters, the first congregation of teaching sisters in the Church.

Angela died on January 27, 1540, when her congregation was still in its beginning stages. Her trust in God had gotten her through many hard tests in her lifetime. There was no doubt in her mind that the Lord would take care of the mission she had begun. And so he did.

Today the Ursuline Sisters have spread to many countries. Angela's sisters continue to work for Jesus and his Church, especially in the education of children and young adults. Angela was proclaimed a saint by Pope Pius VI in 1807.

St. Angela Merici reminds us that our own struggles and disappointments can help us understand the hurts of others. When we are willing to reach out, the Lord will use us to bring his blessings to others. We can ask St. Angela to show us how to be sensitive and compassionate.

January 28

St. Thomas Aquinas

Thomas was born to a noble family around 1225, in Aquino, Italy. When he was five or six years old, his mother and father sent him to the Benedictine Monastery at Monte Cassino to study. In the fall of 1239 he transferred to the University of Naples to continue his education.

In Naples, Thomas met some members of a new religious order called the Order of Preachers. Their founder, St. Dominic, was still living. Thomas knew that he wanted to be a priest, and he felt called to the life being lived by the followers of St. Dominic (soon to become known as the "Dominicans"). Thomas joined the Order of Preachers, but his family was totally against his decision. His brothers even kidnapped him and brought him back to Roccasecca castle. His family kept him there, almost like a prisoner, for about fifteen months, trying to make him change his mind. But Thomas spoke so beautifully about the joy of serving God that *they* finally changed *their* minds and let him go back to the Dominicans!

Thomas rejoined the Order in 1245, and was sent to study at Paris. Even though he was very intelligent, Thomas was always very humble. He never showed off. In fact, his classmates often thought that he was not very bright because he was so quiet in class. Thomas was ordained a priest at Cologne, Germany, in 1250 or 1251.

After his ordination, Thomas began to teach at the University of Paris. He soon became famous for his wonderful teachings about the Bible. Around 1259 he returned to Italy. He continued his work as a teacher there.

During these years Thomas also wrote many books. Some were all about God. Others explained many important things about our Catholic faith. St. Thomas wrote so well that people all over the world still use his books. His explanations about God and the faith came from his great love for God. Thomas was effective because he wasn't trying to make an impression on anyone. He only wanted with all his heart to offer the gift of his life to Jesus and the Church. Even though his intelligence was amazing, Thomas knew that holiness of life was the most important thing. He used to say, "I learn more things from praying before a crucifix than I do from books."

Around the end of 1273, Pope Gregory X asked Thomas to be part of an important Church meeting called the Council of Lyons. While traveling to the meeting, Thomas became ill. He had to stop at a monastery at Fossanova, Italy, where he died. It was March 7, 1274. He was only forty-nine. Thomas Aquinas was canonized a saint in 1323 by Pope Benedict XI. St. Thomas is also a Doctor of the Church and the patron saint of universities, colleges and schools.

All of St. Thomas' learning, writing, and teaching are not what made him a saint. He became a saint by doing everything for God with love. He will help us do the same if we ask him.

January 29

St. Genevieve

Genevieve was born in the small village of Nanterre, near Paris, France, around the year 422.

When she was seven years old, St. Germanus, the bishop of Auxerre, visited her town. After hearing him preach, Genevieve decided to consecrate her life to God.

When Genevieve's parents died, she went to live with her godmother in Paris. She became a nun at the age of fifteen (this was not unusual in those days). Genevieve was very close to God, and God sometimes let her know things that would happen in the future. The people of Paris made fun of her predictions about the future, but Bishop Germanus believed her. When her predictions started to come true, Genevieve's enemies began to believe and respect her.

When Childeric and the Frank army took over Paris, the people suffered very much. Since there was a famine in the city, Genevieve went out with a group of people to look for food. They came back with several boats loaded with corn. Even though Childeric didn't believe in God, he respected Genevieve and spared the lives of many prisoners when she asked him to.

In 451, the people of Paris learned that Attila II and his Huns were headed toward them. In their fear, they decided to leave the city. But Genevieve convinced them to stay. She predicted that if everyone prayed and did penance, Attila and his Huns would pass around Paris, leaving it unharmed. As the people prayed with Genevieve, Attila suddenly changed the direction of his march, and did not invade Paris.

Genevieve died on January 3, 512, at the age of eighty-nine. She was buried in the Church of Saints

Peter and Paul, which she had designed and had convinced King Clovis to build. Because of the many miracles that took place near her tomb, the church was renamed in her honor. St. Genevieve is the patron saint of Paris.

St. Genevieve helped save the people of Paris by her prayers and by her courage in standing up for what was right. One of the best ways for us to help our country is to pray for our leaders. We should ask God to guide them for the good of us all.

January 30

St. Maria Soledad Torres-Acosta

Vibiana Torres-Acosta was born in Madrid, Spain, in 1826. As a child, her mother taught her to love God and his mother Mary. She also became aware of the poor people who were her neighbors, and she did what she could to help them. Vibiana would visit them when they were sick, and offer prayers and sacrifices for them.

When she was older, Vibiana wanted to be a Dominican nun. But the convent was full, and she was placed on a waiting list. In the meantime, she heard about a new religious order of sisters being started by a priest named Father Michael Martinez. He wanted to do something to help the poor who could not afford to go to the hospitals when they got sick. Vibiana decided to ask Father Michael if she could help in his work.

In 1851, at the age of twenty-four, Vibiana and six other young women became the first members of the Congregation of the Sister Servants of Mary. Vibiana received the name Sister Maria Soledad.

The new community met with many hardships. But they were able to carry out their difficult work of taking care of the sick by seeing Jesus himself in their suffering patients. In 1856, a cholera epidemic struck the city of Madrid. Sister Soledad and her sisters worked tirelessly to help its victims. Because of their selflessness and courage in the face of danger, they became well known throughout Spain.

After this, Father Michael left to work in the missions. He named Sister Soledad the superior general of the community before he left. This position of authority did not stop Sister Soledad from helping with the chores, working alongside her sisters as they washed their laundry at the river, gathered firewood, and cooked their simple meals.

As the order grew, the Sister Servants of Mary opened foundations in Europe and the Americas. Sister Soledad died of pneumonia in Madrid in 1887. She was canonized in 1970 by Pope Paul VI.

St. Maria Soledad Torres-Acosta became a great saint by remaining humble and by living a poor

*and simple life. Sometimes we're tempted to want a
lot of things that we really don't need. We can follow the example of St. Maria and think more of the
treasures we will have in heaven.*

January 31

St. John Bosco

John Bosco was born on August 16, 1815, in
Becchi, a small town near Turin, Italy. His parents were
poor farmers. When John was only two years old, his
father died. John's mother struggled to keep the family together. As soon as he was old enough, John began
working as hard as he could to help his mother.

As he grew up, John started to think about
becoming a priest. But he didn't say anything to his
mother because he knew they couldn't afford the
seminary tuition. Besides, his mother needed help to
run their farm. So John waited and prayed and
hoped. Finally, a holy priest named Don Joseph
Cafasso ("Don" is a special title of respect and honor
which people in Italy use for priests) became aware
of John's desire. Don Cafasso helped him enter the
seminary.

John had to work his way through school. He
learned all kinds of trades. He was a carpenter, a shoemaker, a cook, a pastry maker and a farmer. He did
many other jobs as well. He could never have guessed

how much this practical experience would help others later on.

John became a priest in 1841. After his ordination, Don Bosco began working with Don Cafasso visiting the prisons in Turin. He was saddened to see how many boys were in the prisons, and how hopeless their futures were. Don Bosco decided to open a home for troubled boys.

Because of his kindness and caring, it was easy for him to attract youngsters. Don Bosco taught the boys different trades so that they could get good jobs and not be tempted to steal or get into trouble. He prayed with them, and took them on outings. He even organized a brass band! By 1850, there were 150 boys living at his home for boys. Don Bosco's mother was the housekeeper.

At first, people didn't understand what Don Bosco was trying to do. But soon everyone began to realize that he was carrying on a very important work. His boys were learning skills and receiving an education. They were becoming young men who would contribute to society instead of turning to lives of crime. Don Bosco even built a church for the boys. Daily Mass and the sacrament of Reconciliation were the foundation of their whole education.

Don Bosco felt that his success with the boys was due to an attitude of love and respect rather than the use of harsh discipline. Religious instruction and prayer helped the boys *want* to lead good lives.

Don Bosco started his own religious order of priests and brothers too. They were called the Salesians, in honor of St. Francis de Sales. An order of Salesian sisters was started later, with the help of Mary Mazzarello (who also became a saint). When Don Bosco died in Turin on January 31, 1888, there were 250 Salesian houses around the world educating 130,000 children. By the same time, over 6,000 of his boys had chosen to become priests! One of them, Dominic Savio, who became one of Don Bosco's students at the age of twelve, is now a saint too. A young parish priest who had once met Don Bosco later became Pope Pius XI. He had the joy of declaring Don Bosco a saint in 1934.

We can learn from St. John Bosco to use our skills and abilities to help others. What special talents do you have? Think of ways you can use these talents to help those around you. Try to also reach out in friendship to people you may find it hard to like. This is another way to imitate St. John Bosco.

FEBRUARY

February 1

St. Brigid of Ireland

St. Brigid was born around the year 450 in Ireland. Her parents had been baptized by St. Patrick, who brought the faith to that country. Much of what we know about her is from legend.

As Brigid grew up, she grew in her love for Jesus. She looked for him in the poor and often brought food and clothing to them. The story is told that one day she gave away a whole pail of milk. Then she began to worry about what her mother would say. She prayed to the Lord to make up for what she had given away. When she got home, her pail was full again!

As a young girl, Brigid wanted to devote her life to Jesus. She became a nun with the help of St. Mel, St. Patrick's nephew. Bridgid later formed a religious community with seven other young women.

She started the first Irish convent at Kildare and became its abbess. She also founded a school of art, which won fame for its beautifully illuminated manuscripts. The monastery at Kildare became a center of education and spirituality. In time, the city of Kildare with its cathedral grew up around it.

Brigid became known as the "Mary of the Irish" because her love and compassion reminded people of the Blessed Mother. She died in 525 and was buried at Downpatrick near St. Columba and St. Patrick.

Jesus loves each one of us. St. Brigid imitated the love and compassion of Jesus, especially for the poor. She reminds us that every person is special to God.

February 2

Presentation of the Lord

Forty days after Jesus was born, Mary and Joseph brought him to the great Temple in Jerusalem. There they presented Jesus to the Heavenly Father. That was the Jewish law. The Holy Family obeyed it with loving hearts.

While they were in the Temple, Mary also fulfilled another requirement of the law. After the birth of their children, all Jewish mothers were supposed to go to the Temple for the ceremony called the Purification. Mary did her duty cheerfully. She teaches us to be humble and obedient as she was.

A holy old man named Simeon was in the Temple. He had learned from God that the Infant Jesus was truly the Savior. With what joy he held

Mary's Son in his arms. "My own eyes are looking at my salvation!" he exclaimed. God let Simeon recognize Jesus as the Savior, and Simeon put his trust in Jesus. Imagine what Mary and Joseph were thinking. Then, inspired by God, Simeon told Mary that she would have to suffer very much. He was talking about the terrible pain our Blessed Mother would feel when Jesus died on the cross.

This feast of the Presentation reminds us that we belong to God first of all. Because he is our Father and Creator, we owe him our loving obedience.

We, too, can try to be like Mary and Joseph. We can cheerfully obey our parents, guardians and teachers in all that is right. We can ask the Holy Family to help us live in goodness and love.

February 3

St. Blase

St. Blase lived in the fourth century. It is believed that he came from a rich family and received a Christian education. As a young man, Blase became a priest and then bishop of Sebaste in Armenia, which is now modern Turkey. With all his heart, Blase worked to make his people holy and happy. He prayed and preached. He tried to help everyone.

When the governor, Licinius, began persecuting the Christians, Blase went to live and pray and do penance by himself. He became a hermit. In his solitude, wild animals that were sick or hurt would come to him, and he would heal them. One day some hunters found Blase and brought him to the governor. Blase was sent to prison to be beheaded. On the way, people crowded the road to see their beloved bishop for the last time. He blessed them all, even the non-Christians.

Just then, a poor mother rushed up to him. She begged him to save her child who was choking to death on a fishbone. The saint whispered a prayer and blessed the child. He worked a miracle that saved the child's life. That is why St. Blase is called upon by all who have throat diseases. On his feast day, we have our throats blessed at Mass. We ask St. Blase to protect us from all sicknesses of the throat.

While he was in prison, Bishop Blase brought many people to believe in Jesus. No torture could make him give up his faith in Jesus. He was beheaded in the year 316. Now St. Blase is with Jesus forever.

Even on his way to prison, St. Blase was ready to help others. He gave up his life because of his great love for Jesus. When we make little sacrifices such as doing things we don't especially like, or giving up something that we do like, we can think of the happiness we will have in heaven, which will last forever.

February 3 is also the feast of St. Ansgar.

St. Jane Valois

St. Jane was the daughter of King Louis XI of France. She was born in 1464. Since the king wanted a son, he was very disappointed at the birth of Jane. He did not even want his little daughter to live at the palace because she had been born with a physical deformity. When the princess was just five years old, she was sent to live with other people. In spite of the unkind way her father treated her, Jane was good and gentle with everyone. She was convinced that Jesus and Mary loved her. Jane also believed that the Lord would use her to do good in his name. And she was right!

When she grew up, Jane decided that she did not want to get married. She had given herself to Jesus and his Blessed Mother. But her father ignored her wishes. He forced her to marry the duke of Orleans. Jane was a devoted wife for twenty-two years. After the duke became king, however, he sent Jane to live by herself in a far-off township. The queen did not let herself become resentful. Instead, she exclaimed: "God be praised! He has permitted this that I may serve him better than I have up until now."

Jane lived a prayerful life. She practiced penances and acts of kindness. She gave all her money to the poor. She even started an order of sisters called the

Sisters of the Annunciation of the Blessed Virgin Mary. She spent the rest of her life joyfully serving Jesus and his Mother. Jane died in 1505. She was proclaimed a saint by Pope Pius XII in 1950.

When someone treats us unfairly, let's remember that God loves us and that we are precious to him. St. Jane can help us to be as patient and forgiving as she was.

February 5

St. Agatha

Most of what we know about St. Agatha is based on legend. Agatha was a beautiful Christian girl from a wealthy family in Sicily. She lived in the third century, a time when the emperor Decius was persecuting the Christians. While she was still young, she dedicated her life to God, vowing not to get married.

The governor heard of Agatha's beauty and brought her to his palace. He wanted to make her do sinful things, but she was brave and would not give in. "My Lord Jesus Christ," she prayed, "I belong only to you. Help me to be strong against evil."

Then the governor tried sending Agatha to the house of a wicked woman. He hoped the woman would convince Agatha to do sinful things. But Agatha had great trust in God and prayed all the time. She kept herself pure. She would not listen to the evil suggestions of the woman and her daughters. After a month, Agatha was brought back to the governor. "You are a noblewoman," he said kindly. "Why have you lowered yourself to be a humble Christian?"

"Even though I am a noble," answered Agatha, "I am a slave of Jesus Christ."

"Then what does it really mean to be noble?" the governor asked.

Agatha answered, "It means to serve God."

When he realized that Agatha would not agree to the evil he wanted her to do, the governor became angry. He had Agatha whipped and tortured. As she was being carried back to prison she whispered, "Lord, my Creator, you have protected me from the cradle. You have taken me from the love of the world and given me patience to suffer. Now receive my soul."

Agatha died a martyr at Catania, Sicily, in the year 251.

We can learn from St. Agatha's example. Like her, we can pray with all our heart when we are tempted to do anything wrong. This is the way we can develop a good and strong character.

February 6

St. Paul Miki and Companions

These twenty-six martyrs are sometimes called the martyrs of Nagasaki and the martyrs of Japan. St. Francis Xavier brought the Good News of Christianity to Japan in 1549. Many people accepted the Gospel and were baptized by St. Francis himself. Although Francis moved on and eventually died near the shores of China, the Catholic faith continued to grow in Japan. By 1587 there were 200,000 Japanese Catholics. Missionaries from various religious orders were working in the country, and Japanese priests, religious and lay people lived the faith joyfully.

Paul Miki was born at Tounucumada, Japan, in 1562. He was educated by the Jesuits at Anziquiama, and joined their order in 1580. Paul was an excellent preacher and catechist.

In 1588, the emperor of Japan ordered all Jesuits to leave the country within six months. Many stayed, in disguise, because they knew that faithful Catholics would need them, especially during the coming times of persecution.

In 1597, Toyotomi Hideyoshi, who ruled Japan in the emperor's name, heard a false rumor that the missionaries were only bringing Christianity to the Japanese so that it would be easier for Spain and Portugal to defeat Japan. Fearing this was true,

Hideyoshi ordered all the Christians to be arrested and put to death.

On February 5, 1597, Paul Miki was crucified along with two other Japanese Jesuit catechists, six Franciscans from Spain, Mexico and India, and seventeen Japanese Catholic lay people, including children as young as twelve and fifteen. Paul's last words from his cross were to encourage the community of believers to be faithful, even in the face of death. Then, at the same moment, twenty-six executioners thrust twenty-six spears into the Christians as they hung on their crosses.

St. Paul Miki and his companions were canonized as the martyrs of Japan by Pope Gregory XVI in 1862.

We can pray every day for people who live in parts of the world where they are persecuted for their belief in God. We can also ask St. Paul and his companions for the courage to be faithful to Jesus.

February 7

St. Giles Mary

Brother Giles Mary was born near Taranto, Italy, in 1729. As a child he learned the art of rope making and was good at his trade.

When he was twenty-five, Giles entered the Friars of St. Peter Alcántara in Naples. His full religious name was Brother Giles Mary of St. Joseph. Brother Giles Mary became known for his simplicity and humility.

Brother Giles focused all his attention on serving God with love. He was the porter, the one in charge of answering the door of the monastery. Brother Giles opened the door promptly and with a smile every time a visitor pulled the rope that rang the bell. He took gentle care of the poor, the homeless, and the lepers who came asking for help. He was given the responsibility of distributing the food and money that his community could spare. Brother Giles Mary loved to do that. No matter how much he gave to needy people, something was always left to give to others. Brother Giles knew it was St. Joseph who kept him from running out of food and money to give to the poor. After all, St. Joseph had once taken such good care of Jesus and Mary. Brother Giles Mary spent his whole life spreading devotion to St. Joseph.

After a life of love and service to God and his neighbor, Brother Giles Mary of St. Joseph died on February 7, 1812. He was canonized by Pope John Paul II in 1996.

The life of St. Giles shows that it's not great things or important responsibilities that make us "successful" in God's eyes. What pleases God the most is a loving and generous heart.

St. Josephine Bakhita

St. Josephine Bakhita was born in Sudan, Africa, in 1869. When she was a child, she was captured and sold as a slave and suffered harsh treatment. The name "Bakhita," which means "fortunate," was given to her in sarcasm by the people who kidnapped her.

Bakhita was taken to Italy and put into service as a nanny. She was sent to live with the Canossian Sisters in Venice. From the sisters she learned about God and Christianity. In time, she asked to be baptized, and took the name Josephine.

At the age of forty-one, Josephine felt God calling her to become one of the sisters. The Canossian Sisters accepted her into their community. For twenty-five years, Sister Josephine carried out humble services in the convent. She cooked, sewed, took care of the chapel and answered the door. During World War I, Sister Josephine helped to care for the wounded. She became known for her kindness and goodness. She was a source of comfort and encouragement to everyone who came to her in need.

Someone once asked Sister Josephine how she would react if she ever met the people who had kidnapped her. She answered, "I would kiss their hands to thank them for giving me the chance to become a Christian and a sister."

As Sister Josephine grew older, her health began to decline. She continued to live a life of loving kindness and faith even in sickness and pain.

As her death drew near, she said, "Why should I be afraid to die? Death brings us to God, and I love God and want to be with him."

Sister Josephine Bakhita died at the age of seventy-eight. Her last words were "Our Lady! Our Lady!" She was canonized on October 1, 2000, by Pope John Paul II. St. Josephine is the patron saint of the Christian Sudanese people who still suffer persecution for their faith.

Let's learn from St. Josephine Bakhita to put our trust in God when we have problems or when we have something to suffer. God, who loves us without limits, can bring good even out of bad circumstances.

February 8 is also the feast of St. Jerome Emiliani.

St. Apollonia and the Martyrs of Alexandria

A holy woman named Apollonia lived in Alexandria, Egypt, in the third century. Christians were being persecuted there during the reign of Emperor Philip. Apollonia had spent her whole life serving God. Now that she was growing old, she was not about to take time to rest. She bravely risked her life to comfort suffering Christians in prison. "Remember that your trials will not last long," she would say. "But the joys of heaven will last forever."

It was just a matter of time until Apollonia, too, was captured. When the judge asked her name, she courageously said, "I am a Christian, and I love and serve the true God."

Angry people tortured Apollonia, trying to force her to give up her faith. First, all her teeth were smashed and then knocked out. Because of this, St. Apollonia is the patron of dentists. But even this painful ordeal did not shake the woman's faith. Apollonia was then told that if she did not deny Jesus, she would be thrown into a raging fire. The woman would not let her fear overcome her. She chose to die by fire rather than abandon her faith in Jesus. When the pagans saw how heroic she was, many were converted to faith in Jesus. Apollonia died around the year 249.

St. Apollonia and the other martyrs were willing to give up their lives for Jesus. What are we willing to do for him? Do we love Jesus enough to accept a little inconvenience without complaining?

February 10

St. Scholastica

St. Scholastica and St. Benedict were twins born in central Italy in 480. When they grew up, Benedict founded an order of monks called the Benedictines. Scholastica wanted to dedicate herself to God also, so she began a community of nuns near her brother's monastery of Monte Cassino.

Scholastica and Benedict decided that they would only visit each other once a year as a sacrifice to show their love for God. They used to meet at a house near their monasteries. When it was time to visit Benedict in 547, God let Scholastica know that it would be the last time they saw each other on earth. Because of this, she wanted to stay and talk longer than usual, but her brother said no. According to their Rule of Life, Benedict had to go back to his monastery at night, and Scholastica had to return to hers.

Since Benedict would not give in, Scholastica quietly turned to God in prayer. All of a sudden, a terrible storm began. Thunder crashed overhead, light-

Our Lady of Lourdes

ning lit up the sky, and rain poured down in sheets. It was impossible to step out of the house!

Benedict asked in surprise, "Sister, what have you done?"

"Since you would not give me the favor I asked," Scholastica calmly replied, "I asked God to give it to me, and he did."

The brother and sister spent that whole night talking about God and heaven. In the morning, after the storm had ended, they each went home. Three days later, St. Scholastica died. At the same time, in his own monastery, Benedict was praying. He saw the soul of his sister flying up to heaven like a dove.

St. Scholastica and St. Benedict helped each other draw closer to God by the way they treated one another. Our parents, guardians, teachers and good friends can all help us to become closer to God.

February 11

Our Lady of Lourdes

It was on February 11, 1858, that a beautiful Lady first appeared to Bernadette Soubirous in the small town of Lourdes, France. Bernadette had asthma and was often sick. Her family was so poor that they were living in a cold, damp room that had once been a jail. Even though she was fourteen, Bernadette still could not read or write. She had a bad memory and never could remember her religious instruction lessons, but she loved God very much. She tried to learn all that she could about God, and she tried even harder to please him.

The beautiful Lady Bernadette saw appeared in a grotto, a kind of natural cave carved into a rocky cliff. She wore a white dress and a light blue sash. A white veil covered her head and fell over her shoulders to the ground. On her feet were two lovely golden roses. Her hands were joined and a rosary hung from her right arm. Its chain and cross shone like gold. The lovely Lady encouraged Bernadette to pray the rosary. The Lady appeared eighteen times to Bernadette. She asked her to tell the people to pray, to do penance and to recite the rosary, especially for sinners.

At first, people did not believe Bernadette was seeing a beautiful Lady at the grotto, because they could see no one. But soon large crowds began to follow her to the site. On February 25, the Lady pointed to a spot nearby and told Bernadette to scratch at the ground. A spring of water began to flow. This spring still flows freely, and many people go there to ask for healing!

During the last apparition, on March 25, 1858, Bernadette asked the beautiful Lady her name. The Lady replied, "I am the Immaculate Conception." Bernadette did not understand what this meant. She hurried to tell her pastor. The priest understood. This name meant that the Lady was Mary, the Mother of God!

Bernadette entered the convent in 1866. She lived a hidden, humble life until her death on April 16, 1879.

Three beautiful churches have been built at different levels on the rocky cliff where Bernadette saw the Blessed Mother. Although the apparitions took place over 150 years ago, miracles still happen there. Many people are cured of sicknesses. Some crippled people walk again. Some blind people see again. But more importantly, people have their faith in God renewed and receive many spiritual graces. At Lourdes, where she once appeared to St. Bernadette, our Lady still shows her love for all of us.

Let's try to say the rosary to our Blessed Mother every day, just as St. Bernadette did. Through this prayer, we receive all the graces we need for ourselves and for those we love.

February 12

St. Meletius

Meletius lived in the fourth century. The Roman persecutions were over, and Emperor Constantine had recognized Christianity as a legal religion in 315. But a serious problem was dividing Christians. While most people considered themselves Catholic, others were Arian. The Arians denied that Jesus is

God. They taught that he was only a holy man. Some people believed this false teaching because they were very confused.

Meletius loved the Church and was true to Jesus. He knew and believed that Jesus *is* God, and he was not afraid to teach this. Meletius realized that the Church needed to explain this truth to everyone. Meletius became the bishop of Antioch in 361. The Arians were not pleased. For twenty years, Meletius was a patient, loving bishop. But his life was made difficult by people who did not accept him. He often had to go into exile because other men were claiming to be the bishop of his diocese. But St. Meletius was the true bishop and would patiently return as soon as possible. When Emperor Valens died in 378, the Arians finally stopped their persecution.

In 381, the famous Council of Constantinople, a special Church meeting, was called. The bishops wanted to talk about important truths of our faith. Bishop Meletius opened the council meetings and directed the sessions. Then, to the sadness of all the bishops, he died right there at one of the meetings.

Great saints like John Chrysostom and Gregory of Nyssa attended his funeral along with all the bishops at the Council. The people of Constantinople poured into the church as well. St. Gregory of Nyssa delivered the funeral homily. He spoke of Bishop Meletius' calmness and radiant smile, his fatherly voice and gentleness. St. Gregory said that Meletius was a Christ-like bishop whom everyone loved. And he was right: everyone who loved the Church loved St. Meletius.

St. Meletius was always kind and good-natured. Many people made his life difficult, but he never lost his gentle ways. This is how he proved his love for Jesus. Let's try to be kind even to those who are not kind to us.

February 13

St. Catherine of Ricci

Alexandrina was born in 1522 into the Ricci family of Florence, Italy. When she was about thirteen years old, she entered the Dominican order. (Girls could become sisters at a very young age in those days.) Her new name was Sister Catherine.

Sister Catherine loved Jesus very much. She used to think a lot about the sufferings he went through for all of us. From the time she was twenty until she was thirty-two years old, Jesus let her have visions of what his crucifixion was like. This happened every week. Jesus also gave Catherine the great privilege of receiving in her own body the marks of his wounds. This special gift is called the *stigmata.* Sister Catherine was happy to share in the sufferings of Jesus.

Catherine also felt very sorry for those people who have died but are not yet ready to live with God in heaven. Their souls must be purified or made clean before they can see God. This happens in *purgatory*. Sister Catherine prayed and did penance for the souls in purgatory.

When Catherine was thirty, she was elected the superior of her convent for life. She devoted her time to prayer, to assisting those who came to her for advice, and to helping the sick and the poor.

Sister Catherine died at the age of sixty-eight, after a long, painful illness. It was February 2, 1590. She was proclaimed a saint by Pope Clement XII in 1747.

We can help the souls in purgatory with our prayers just as St. Catherine did. We can pray that they soon may be with the Lord. When they are in heaven, they will pray for us.

February 14

St. Cyril and St. Methodius

These two brothers were from Thessalonica, Greece. Methodius was born in 815 and Cyril in 827. Both became priests and shared the same holy desire to spread the Catholic faith.

In 861, Emperor Michael III asked Cyril and Methodius to travel to Russia to teach the people about Jesus. The brothers learned the Russian language so that they could use it to explain the Gospel. Many people in Russia understood the message of Jesus because they heard it in their own language from Cyril and Methodius. Many asked to be baptized.

Two years later Prince Rostislav of Moravia (today part of the Czech Republic) asked the two brothers to come to bring the good news of Christ to his land. This time they used the Slavonic language in preaching and in the liturgy, because it was the language the Moravians could understand.

Some people at that time thought that it was wrong to use the language of the people instead of the Latin language in Church services. They complained about Cyril and Methodius and the two brothers were called to Rome by Pope Adrian II. But the Pope was so pleased with their good work in telling others about Christ, that he gave his approval and said that Cyril and Methodius should be made bishops.

Cyril died soon after this in 869, and we don't know if he was ever consecrated a bishop. But Methodius was, and he went back to Moravia. The last part of his life was spent finishing a translation of the Bible, a work he had begun with Cyril. Methodius died in 885. He and Cyril are known as the apostles to the Slavs. On December 31, 1980, Pope John Paul II declared St. Cyril and St. Methodius co-patrons of Europe along with St. Benedict.

We can learn a lot from the generosity of St. Cyril and St. Methodius. We can also ask them to help us be respectful of all people even if their religion, customs, language and culture may be different from our own.

Also traditionally remembered on February 14:

St. Valentine

Valentine was a holy priest who lived in Rome in the third century. When Emperor Claudius II banned Christianity, Valentine helped and encouraged the Christians who faced martyrdom rather than give up their faith. It is said he even performed marriage ceremonies for Christian couples.

Then Valentine himself was arrested. When he refused to give up his faith and worship the pagan Roman gods, he was put in prison. According to one legend, the official who imprisoned him had a blind daughter. Valentine cured her, and the official's whole family became Christian. When Valentine was condemned to death, he wrote a farewell letter to the girl and signed it, "from your Valentine." This could be where we get the custom of sending "Valentines" on February 14.

St. Valentine was beheaded on February 14 in the year 269 or 270. He was buried on the Flaminian Road, where a basilica, a large and beautiful church, was built in 350.

Some people think the custom of sending valentines grew from a belief in the Middle Ages that birds began to choose their mates on February 14. But the best reason for honoring St. Valentine as the patron saint of love is his own great love of God, which never weakened—even at the cost of his life.

February 15

St. Faustinus and St. Jovita

St. Faustinus and St. Jovita were brothers who lived in Brescia, Italy. They were among the early Christian martyrs. The two brothers suffered during the persecution of Emperor Hadrian in the second century.

From the time they were young, Faustinus and Jovita were well known for their great love for their religion. They also performed works of Christian charity. They helped each other do good for the people who needed them. Faustinus was a priest; Jovita was a deacon. They began to preach everywhere, to both the rich and the poor. They spared themselves no sacrifice to bring many people to God. Because it was a time of persecution, it was easy to be afraid. But Faustinus and Jovita would not give in to fear of the soldiers even though these soldiers were actually putting many Christians to death.

When the emperor heard that Faustinus and Jovita dared to preach openly about Jesus, he sent them to prison and had them tortured. He hoped that torture would stop them from teaching about Jesus. But the emperor was wrong. No matter what the two priests suffered, they would not promise to stop preaching about Jesus. They prayed and offered all their sufferings to the Lord. Faustinus and Jovita encouraged each other to be courageous even if they, too, would have to die as martyrs for Jesus.

Both brothers remained true to their belief in and love for Jesus until they were martyred. The exact date of their death was not recorded, but the Church remembers their heroic example.

God is very pleased to see brothers and sisters helping one another to study and learn about their faith. Like St. Faustinus and St. Jovita, they can encourage each other to love and live for Jesus.

February 16

St. Onesimus

Onesimus lived in the first century. He was a young slave who stole something from his master and then ran away to Rome. In Rome he went to see the great apostle, St. Paul, who was in prison for preaching about Jesus. Paul welcomed Onesimus with kindness and helped him realize that he had done wrong to steal. But more than that, Paul led Onesimus to believe in and accept the Christian faith. After Onesimus became a Christian, Paul sent him back to his master, Philemon, who was Paul's friend. But Paul did not send the slave back alone and defenseless. He "armed" Onesimus with a brief, powerful letter. Paul hoped his letter would set everything right for his new friend, Onesimus. Paul wrote to Philemon: "I plead with you for my own son, for Onesimus. I am sending him back to you. Welcome him as though he were my very heart."

That touching letter is now in the New Testament of the Bible. Philemon accepted Paul's letter and Paul's advice. When Onesimus returned, Philemon set him free. Later, Onesimus went back to St. Paul and became his faithful helper.

St. Paul made Onesimus a priest and then a bishop. The former slave dedicated the rest of his life to preaching the Good News that had changed his life forever.

If we ever hurt anyone in any way, let's ask forgiveness right away. God will be pleased to see that we're sorry and he will bless us as he blessed Onesimus.

Seven Founders of the Order of Servites

In the thirteenth century in the city of Florence, Italy, seven young men formed a group called the Praisers of Mary. They met in order to pray, and they were especially devoted to Mary.

The way they came to be founders of the Servite Order is remarkable. On the feast of the Assumption, while the seven friends were deep in prayer, the Blessed Mother appeared to them. She inspired them to leave everything behind and to live alone with God. After several years of living as hermits, they went to their bishop. They asked him for a rule of life to follow. The bishop encouraged them to pray and to ask for guidance from Mary. Mary again appeared to the men. This time she was carrying a black habit (a kind of robe). At her side was an angel holding a scroll with the words "Servants of Mary" written on it. In this vision, the Blessed Mother said that she had chosen them to be her servants. She asked them to wear a black habit. This was the habit they started to wear in 1240. They also began to live their religious life according to the rule of St. Augustine.

The seven founders' names are Bonfilius, Bonajuncta, Amideus, Hugh, Manettus, Sostenes, and

Alexius. All of them except Alexius became priests. Alexius felt himself unworthy to be ordained.

Others joined the group and the Servite Order grew. The purpose of the members was to become more and more like Jesus, to preach the Gospel, and to spread devotion to Mary, especially as Our Lady of Sorrows. The Servite Order was approved by the Vatican in 1259. The seven holy founders were declared saints by Pope Leo XIII in 1888.

Like these seven saints, let's love our Blessed Mother and ask her to help us in every need.

February 18

Blessed Elisabetta Canori-Mora

Elisabetta was born in Rome in 1774 into a well-to-do Christian family. When she was eleven years old, she began attending school with the Augustinian nuns. She was a student with the nuns for three years. She became very close to God during this time.

When she was twenty-two, Elisabetta married a lawyer named Cristoforo Mora. They had four children, but two of them died when they were very young. Cristoforo turned out to be a cruel husband. He mistreated Elisabetta. After a while, he left home. Now Elisabetta had to care for her two children all by herself.

Elisabetta lived in poverty. She worked as a maid and took in sewing and laundry to earn some money. Besides having to provide for her children, she also had to pay Cristoforo's debts. But this did not keep Elisabetta from reaching out to those who had even less than she did. She shared what little she had with the poor and took care of the sick. The doors to her home were always open to anyone who needed her help. Because she was a deeply prayerful woman, she was a source of peace and faith for the discouraged and hopeless.

Instead of holding a grudge against her husband, Elisabetta prayed for him and offered up her sufferings for his conversion. After her death in 1825, Cristoforo was touched by God's grace. He repented of his sins and eventually became a priest.

Elisabetta was beatified on April 24, 1994 by Pope John Paul II.

Blessed Elisabetta faced many difficulties in her life. But they didn't make her bitter or self-centered. Instead, she asked herself what she could do to make life easier for others. When someone is unkind to us, we can ask Blessed Elisabetta to help us be kind and forgiving instead of holding a grudge.

St. Barbatus

Barbatus was born in Benevento, Italy, in 612. He took his faith seriously and especially liked to read the Bible. As soon as he was old enough, Barbatus was ordained a priest. Later he was made a pastor. But his life as a pastor was not easy. Some people did not like it when Father Barbatus encouraged them to lead better lives or when he reminded them to be sorry for their sins. Some of the people got angry. They persecuted him and finally forced him to leave the parish.

The young priest felt badly. He went back to Benevento where he had been born. He was received with great joy. But there were challenges in that city, too. Many converts to Christianity still kept pagan idols in their homes. They found it hard to destroy their good luck charms. They believed in magical powers. Father Barbatus preached against these superstitions. But the people hung on to their false gods. Barbatus warned them that because of this sin, their city would be attacked by enemies. And it was.

Afterward, the people gave up their error and peace returned. Father Barbatus was made bishop. He continued his work to convert his people. He died on February 29, 682, at the age of seventy.

Good parish priests, like St. Barbatus, will challenge us to live according to the teachings of Jesus. Let's listen to their advice and follow it.

February 20

St. Margaret of Cortona

Margaret was the daughter of a farmer in the Tuscany region of Italy. Her mother died when she was only seven years old, and her stepmother treated her harshly. When she was about sixteen, she ran away from home to live with a wealthy young man. They had a son and lived a life of luxury. Nine years after she went to live with him, the man was murdered. Margaret realized the life of sin she had been leading, and decided to change. She was twenty-five years old.

Margaret went to the church at Cortona and confessed in front of everyone the sins she had committed. She and her son were taken in by two ladies in the town, and Margaret joined the Franciscan Third Order. Two Franciscan friars became her spiritual directors. They helped her through three difficult years of discouragement and troubles in prayer. They also tried to make sure that Margaret's penances were not too severe. Because she was so sorry for the wrong things she had done, Margaret wanted to make up for her sins by fasting and performing other acts of self-denial.

After some time spent living all alone, Margaret devoted herself to the poor and the sick. In 1286 she received the bishop's approval to form a community of women who would care for the sick. She founded a hospital for this purpose.

Because of her holiness of life, many people came to her from all over Italy, France and Spain to ask her advice on spiritual matters. God worked many miracles of healing through her, and she was able to help many people to be sorry for their sins. St. Margaret died at Cortona in 1297.

Instead of becoming discouraged when we do something wrong, we can be like St. Margaret and try to do better next time because we want to show our love for God.

February 21

St. Peter Damian

St. Peter Damian was born in 1007, in Ravenna, Italy. He was left an orphan as a little child. An older brother brought Peter to live with him, but he treated him as a servant and sent him to take care of the pigs. After some time, another brother named Damian, who was a priest, found out how Peter was being treated. He took over Peter's care and treated him with love and kindness. Peter was so grateful to his brother Father Damien that he added the name "Damian" to his own name. Father Damian educated Peter and encouraged him in his studies. When Peter grew up, he became a teacher. He was very good at his work, but God had other plans for him.

Peter Damian lived at a time when many people in the Church were forgetting that we are all called to live like Jesus. Peter wanted the Church to shine with the holiness of Jesus. After seven years of teaching, Peter made the decision to become a monk. He would live the rest of his life in prayer and penance so that many people in the Church would become holy. In 1035, Peter Damian went to a monastery of St. Romuald. There he wrote a rule for the monks. He also wrote a life of St. Romuald. Twice his abbot sent him to neighboring monasteries. Peter helped the monks to change their way of life and become closer to God. The monks were grateful because Peter was so kind and respectful. Around 1043, the monks elected Peter abbot. He continually encouraged his monks to live in imitation of Jesus.

In 1057, Pope Stephen IX named Peter cardinal-bishop of Ostia. Throughout his long life, several popes sent Peter on missions to straighten out Church affairs in different places. He also wrote many books explaining the teachings of the Church.

Peter Damian died in 1072 at the age of eighty-three. Because he did so much to spread the truth of the Gospel, Pope Leo XII declared him a Doctor of the Church in 1828.

Even though his older brother was unkind to him when he was growing up, St. Peter Damian trusted in God's love and help. And God took care of him. Let's ask St. Peter to let us know how much God loves us too.

February 22

Chair of St. Peter

The feast of the Chair of St. Peter has been celebrated in Rome since the fourth century. It is a reminder to us that St. Peter established the Christian community in Rome. The chair is a symbol of authority, since a king rules from his throne. But where did St. Peter's authority come from?

In the Gospel, we read how Jesus told Peter, "You are Peter, and on this rock I will build my church" (Mt. 16:18). Jesus knew that when he ascended back to his Father in heaven, his Church on earth would need a leader and guide. Jesus chose Peter to carry out this important mission. Peter would be the chief shepherd of the flock of Jesus. In John's Gospel, the risen Jesus asks Peter three times, "Do you love me?" And just as the weak Peter denied knowing Jesus three times the night before he died, the Peter strengthened by faith in the resurrection declared three times, "Yes, Lord. You know that I love you!" And three times, Jesus told Peter, "Feed my lambs. Tend my sheep. Feed my sheep." (See John 21:15-17.)

The bishops of the Church are like shepherds taking care of their flocks. At first, Peter cared for God's people in Jerusalem and in Antioch, two big cities of the east. Later, he went to preach the Gospel in Rome, the capital of the world. St. Peter was the first bishop of the Church in Rome. After he was martyred, a new bishop was chosen to take his place. From the beginning of the Church until today, there has been an unbroken line of bishops following St. Peter as the bishop of the Church of Rome. And because Jesus put Peter in charge of all his followers, Peter and his successors have also been the leaders of the whole Church throughout the world. The bishop of Rome is called by a special name. We call him the pope.

On this day, we should try to pray more for our Holy Father the pope, who leads and guides the Church with the authority that Jesus gave St. Peter.

We love and honor the pope because he takes the place of Jesus on earth. Let's always pray for our Holy Father. We ask that God may give him strength, light and comfort.

February 23

St. Polycarp

Polycarp was born around the year 75. He became a Christian when there were still not many followers of Jesus. In fact, Polycarp was a disciple of one of the original apostles, St. John. All that Polycarp learned from St. John he taught to others. Polycarp became a priest and then bishop of Smyrna in present-day Turkey. He was Smyrna's bishop for many years. The Christians recognized him as a holy, brave shepherd.

Christians in Polycarp's time faced persecution and death under Emperor Marcus Aurelius. Someone betrayed Polycarp to the authorities. When his captors came to arrest him, Polycarp invited them to first share a meal with him. Then he asked them to let him pray awhile. When he was brought to trial, the judge tried to force Bishop Polycarp to save himself from death by cursing Jesus. "I have served Jesus all my life," answered Polycarp, "and he has never done me any wrong. How can I curse my King who died for me?"

After he had said this, the soldiers tied Polycarp's hands behind his back. The old bishop was then placed on a burning pile. But the fire did not harm him. One of the soldiers then thrust a lance into his heart. And so, in the year 155, when he was eighty years old, Polycarp died a martyr. He went to live forever with Jesus, the Divine Master whom he had served so bravely.

St. Polycarp chose to die rather than curse Jesus. We have many choices to make every day too. If we want to be good and strong Christians like Polycarp we will choose to watch only good TV shows and other media, listen to good music, and be careful about the kinds of books and magazines we read. Our choices will also determine the kind of language we use and the way we treat our family and friends. The choices we make are very important.

February 24

Blessed Josefa Naval Girbes

Josefa was born on December 11, 1820, in a town near Valencia in Spain. When her mother died in 1833, Josefa took over the running of the household. When she was eighteen, she joined the Carmelite Third Order and took a private vow of chastity, promising never to get married.

Josefa offered embroidery classes in her home. As she taught the girls the art of embroidery, she also taught them about God. She prayed with her pupils and encouraged them to lead holy lives. Because of her good example and the wonderful things she taught them about the Lord, many of the young women who took her embroidery classes were inspired to enter the religious life. As Pope John Paul II said at her beatification, "her students filled the cloistered convents while she followed her vocation as an unmarried woman in the world."

In 1885, a cholera epidemic broke out. Josefa bravely and selflessly brought relief and comfort to the sick and dying. Josefa's love of neighbor was a direct result of her love of God. God allowed Josefa to become very, very close to him.

Josefa died on February 24, 1893. She was beatified on September 25, 1988, by Pope John Paul II.

No matter what walk of life God has called us to, we are all called to become saints. Like Blessed Josefa, we can witness to Jesus and lead lives of prayer and goodness wherever we are or whatever we're doing.

February 25

St. Caesarius of Nazianzen

Caesarius lived in the fourth century in the area that is today the country of Turkey. His father was the bishop of Nazianzen. (At that time bishops and priests could be married.) Caesarius' brother is St. Gregory of Nazianzen (Gregory's feast day is January 2).

Both Caesarius and Gregory received an excellent education. Gregory wanted to become a priest, and

Caesarius wanted to become a doctor. The two brothers went to the schools that would help them reach their goals.

Caesarius completed his studies in medicine at Constantinople. He soon became a well-known and trusted doctor. In fact, Emperor Constantius, who lived in Constantinople, wanted Caesarius to be his personal physician. Caesarius thanked the emperor but kindly refused. He wanted to go back to Nazianzen, his home city.

Some time later, however, Caesarius was called to serve the new emperor at Constantinople. This emperor is known in history as Julian the Apostate. (An apostate was someone who gave up the Christian faith.) Emperor Julian had issued several official orders against the Christians. He knew that Caesarius was a Christian, but he liked him because he was such a good doctor. Julian tried to talk Caesarius into giving up his faith. He even offered him bribes and privileges. But Caesarius remained faithful. He followed the advice of his father and brother and went back to Nazianzen.

In 368, Caesarius was almost killed in an earthquake. He escaped unharmed but was badly shaken by the incident. He felt that God was telling him to live a life of prayer away from the noise and flattery of the court. Caesarius gave away his possessions to the poor. He began to live a quiet, prayerful life.

St. Caesarius died shortly after in 369. His brother, St. Gregory, preached the homily at his funeral.

We all have a special call or vocation to follow in life. God has given us the gifts we need to live that vocation. Like St. Caesarius, we need the wisdom to listen to people we trust. We also need to refuse to follow people who want us to use our talents or education in wrong ways.

February 26

St. Porphyry

Porphyry was born in 353 to wealthy, noble parents. He left his family when he was twenty-five. Porphyry went to Egypt to enter a monastery. After five years, he made a trip to Jerusalem. He wanted to visit the places where Jesus had actually been while he was on earth. Porphyry was very impressed by the Holy Land. His love for Jesus made him more deeply aware of the sufferings of the poor. At home in Thessalonica he had never known what it was like to be poor. Now he still owned all that his parents had left him. But not for long. He asked his friend Mark to go to Thessalonica and sell everything for him. After three months, Mark returned with the money. Porphyry then gave it away to those who really needed it.

At the age of forty, Porphyry became a priest. He was given care of the relics of the true cross of Jesus. Porphyry was then made bishop of Gaza. He worked generously to lead the people to believe in Jesus. But

SAINT GABRIEL POSSENTI

JESU XPI
PASSIO

his labors were slow and required heroic patience. At that time most of the people of Gaza followed pagan practices and superstitions. Although Porphyry was able to stop many of these practices, he had enemies who made him suffer greatly.

Others who were Christians loved and admired him deeply. They prayed and sacrificed for him. They begged the Lord to preserve him. Bishop Porphyry spent many years strengthening the Christian community. He was never afraid to teach others about Jesus. He died in 420.

The story of St. Porphyry teaches us that we should not be superstitious and believe in things such as good luck charms. God is the one who watches over us and gives us all the help we need, if we ask him.

February 27

St. Gabriel Possenti

This saint was born in Assisi, Italy, in 1838. He received the name Francis at baptism, in honor of the great St. Francis of Assisi. His mother died when he was only four. Francis's father sent for a governess to raise him and the other children.

Francis grew to be very handsome and likable. He was often the most popular person at a party. He loved to have fun, but there was another side to him, too. Even while having good times, he was sometimes bored. He couldn't explain why. He seemed to feel in his heart a strong desire for God and the deeper things of life.

Twice Francis became so sick that he nearly died. Each time he promised our Lady that if she would obtain his cure, he would become a religious. He did get better both times, but he didn't keep his promise.

One day, he saw a picture of the Sorrowful Mother that was being carried in a procession. It seemed that the Blessed Mother was looking straight at him. At the same time, he heard a voice in his heart telling him, "Francis, the world is not for you anymore."

That did it. Francis entered the Passionist monastery. He was eighteen years old. The new name he took was Gabriel of Our Lady of Sorrows. Gabriel's great loves became the Holy Eucharist and Mary, the Sorrowful Mother. He loved to spend time thinking about the passion of Jesus and how much the Lord had suffered for him. Gabriel also learned to practice two virtues in a special way: humility and obedience. His special trademark was joy. He was always happy, and he spread happiness to those around him. After only a few short years in the Passionist Order, Gabriel died on February 27, 1862. He was proclaimed a saint by Pope Benedict XV in 1920.

Trying to have only good times will leave us empty and dissatisfied. True happiness comes from living according to God's plan. We can ask St. Gabriel to help us find real joy and meaning in our lives.

St. Romanus and St. Lupicinus

These French saints were brothers who lived in the fifth century. As a young man, Romanus was admired by everyone for his goodness. He had a great desire to become a saint. Since he saw that in the world it was too easy to forget about God, Romanus decided to live as a hermit. First, he asked the advice of a holy monk, and then he started off. He took a book with him. It was *The Lives of the Fathers of the Desert* by Cassian. He also took along seeds to plant and a few tools. With these supplies, he went into the forests of the Jura Mountains between Switzerland and France. Romanus found a huge fir tree and settled beneath it. He spent his time praying and reading. He also planted and cared for his garden, quietly enjoying nature.

Soon afterward, his brother Lupicinus joined him. The two brothers were very different. Romanus was hard on himself. However, he was kind and gentle and full of understanding with others. Lupicinus was demanding with himself and usually the same with others. But he meant well. The two brothers understood each other and got along fine.

Many men came to join them. They wanted to be monks, too, so they built two monasteries. Romanus was the abbot of one and Lupicinus was the abbot of the other. The monks lived simple, hard lives. They prayed much and made sacrifices cheerfully. They performed penances to strengthen themselves in their vocation. They had a farm and worked very hard growing their own food. They kept silent all the time so that they could listen to and speak to God.

Romanus died in 460. His younger brother, Lupicinus, died in 480.

St. Romanus and St. Lupicinus were both saints, even though they had different personalities. God gave each of us our own unique personality, which makes us different from any other person on earth.

MARCH

March 1

St. David of Wales

David was the son of King Xantus of South Wales. When he grew up, he became a priest. He went to the Isle of Wight to live as a hermit, with a wise and holy man named Paulinus as his spiritual guide. He lived in solitude for a long time, preparing himself to carry out his ministry.

Then David went out and devoted his life to preaching. He built twelve monasteries and gave the monks a rule, which was based on the lifestyle of the Egyptian monks. The rule encouraged the monks to devote themselves to hard work in the fields and to pray at all times, either with words, or by turning their minds and hearts to God. After their work was done, the monks would return to their monastery to pray, read, and write.

David was asked to attend an important meeting of bishops at Brevi. His wisdom and preaching made such a good impression on the bishops, that he was made a bishop himself. As bishop, David called another meeting in which he set up regulations for the churches in Britain.

David died in the middle of the sixth century, in one of his monasteries. He is the patron saint of Wales.

St. David understood the importance of talking to God. Before beginning his important work of preaching the Gospel, he prepared himself by a long period of prayer and solitude. Before we begin each day, we should take time to ask God for the help we'll need to do well whatever will be asked of us that day. The more we trust in God's help, the more successful we'll be.

March 2

St. Agnes of Bohemia

Princess Agnes was born in 1205. She was the daughter of King Ottokar of Bohemia. At the age of three she was promised in marriage to a nobleman named Boleslaus. (This is how things were done in those days.) Then Boleslaus died, and when Agnes was nine, it was arranged that her future husband would be Emperor Frederick II's son, Henry. But Agnes had secretly promised to live only for God. She wanted to be a nun. So when Henry ignored the marriage arrangement and married the Duke of Austria's daughter instead, Agnes was very happy.

But then Agnes's brother promised her in marriage to Frederick, and in 1235, the wedding plans were started. Agnes asked Pope Gregory IX to help her, explaining that she wanted to become a nun. The pope interceded for her, and she was released from the arranged marriage.

The following year, Agnes built a convent in Prague. St. Clare of Assisi sent five of her nuns to live in the convent, and Agnes joined them. She later became abbess and lived a life of humility, poverty, and kindness to the poor. She died on March 2, 1282.

If we pray to know our vocation in life, God will reveal it to us, as he revealed her vocation to St. Agnes. While parents shouldn't try to force their children into a particular profession or way of life, they can offer helpful advice to guide them in making the right decisions.

March 3

St. Katharine Drexel

Katharine Drexel was born in Philadelphia, Pennsylvania, on November 26, 1858. Her mother died when she was just a baby. Not long after, her father, a very successful banker, got married again to a kind woman named Emma. Emma was very loving to Katharine and her older sister Elizabeth. In a few years another baby girl was born into the family. Mr.

and Mrs. Drexel named her Louise. The three Drexel sisters had a great time growing up together.

Katharine's parents were very religious. The family prayed together every day before an altar they had set up in their home. Mrs. Drexel devoted much of her time to helping the poor, and Katharine and her sisters learned from her the joy of sharing their wealth with those who were in need. This was how they could show their love for God.

When Katharine grew up, she was a very active Catholic. She was generous with her time and her money. She realized that the Church had many needs. She directed her energies and her fortune to helping the poor and forgotten. Her work for Jesus would be among the African American and Native American people.

In 1891, Katharine began a new religious community of missionaries. They were called the Sisters of the Blessed Sacrament. Katharine became known as Mother Katharine.

Mother Katharine inherited her family's great fortune. She used the money for wonderful works of charity. She and her sisters built schools, convents and churches. In 1915, they established Xavier University in New Orleans. During her long, fruitful lifetime, Mother Katharine spent millions of dollars of her inheritance to provide education and assistance to African Americans and Native Americans who were in need. She found Jesus truly present in the Eucharist and in all the people whom she so lovingly served.

Mother Katharine died on March 3,1955, at the age of ninety-seven. She was declared "blessed" by Pope John Paul II on November 20, 1988, and canonized on October 1, 2000. She is the second native-born United States citizen to be declared a saint.

St. Katharine teaches us a special lesson. We could spend our lives being concerned only about ourselves and our own needs. But how much better it is to imitate Mother Katharine and do as much as we can to help others. This will make us more like Jesus!

March 4

St. Casimir

Casimir was born in Cracow, Poland, on October 3, 1458. He was the third of thirteen children born to Casimir IV, king of Poland, and Elizabeth of Austria.

From his childhood, Casimir was taught to live a life of holiness and charity. He preferred to wear plain clothes rather than the fine garments a prince was expected to wear. He spent time each day in prayer, and devoted himself to penance. He got into the habit of always remembering that he was in God's presence. Because of this, he was cheerful and kind to everyone. He was especially devoted to the sufferings of Jesus, to the Holy Mass, and to the Blessed

Virgin Mary. In her honor, he recited a beautiful hymn very often. The name of the hymn is "Daily, Daily, Sing to Mary." His hand-written copy of this hymn was buried with him.

When he was thirteen, Casimir's father pressured him to lead an army against the king of nearby Hungary and seize the throne, making himself the king. But Casimir was convinced that he had no right to do it, so he refused. Casimir was never healthy, yet he was courageous and strong in character. He always did what he knew was right. Sometimes he would even advise his father, the king, to rule the people fairly. He did this with great respect, and his father listened to him.

Casimir's parents found a very beautiful and virtuous young woman for him to marry. But Casimir chose to remain single. He wanted to give his heart to God alone.

While in Lithuania on an assignment of service for that country, Casimir became ill with tuberculosis. He died at the age of twenty-six. He was proclaimed a saint by Pope Leo X in 1521. St. Casimir is the patron of Poland and Lithuania.

St. Casimir helps us see that even if we are not physically strong or healthy, we can still be strong in character. We can always stand up for what is right, but in a kind and respectful way.

St. John Joseph of the Cross

St. John Joseph of the Cross was born in southern Italy on the feast of the Assumption, August 15, 1654. He was a young noble, but he dressed like a poor man. He did that because he wanted to be as poor as Jesus had been.

At the age of sixteen, John Joseph entered the Franciscan Order. He wanted very much to live in imitation of Jesus. This led him to cheerfully make many sacrifices.

Later he was ordained a priest. Father John Joseph became the superior at Santa Lucia's in Naples where he spent most of his long life. He always insisted on doing the hardest work. He happily chose to do the duties that no one else wanted.

John Joseph had a wonderful personality. But he did not try to be the center of attention. Instead of expecting people to recognize his gifts and reach out to him, he would reach out to others. All the priests and brothers thought of him as a loving father. He was very devoted to the Blessed Virgin, and tried to help others love her.

This good priest loved God so much that even when he was sick, he kept on working. Father John Joseph died in March of 1734, at the age of eighty. He was proclaimed a saint by Pope Pius VIII in 1839.

St. John Joseph was generous with his love for God and other people. He invites us to overcome any selfishness we may sometimes feel. Let's really try to treat everyone with the same respect and kindness, even if we might like some people better than others.

March 6

St. Colette

Born in 1381, Nicolette was named in honor of St. Nicholas of Myra. Her parents nicknamed her Colette from the time she was a baby. Colette's father was a carpenter at an abbey in Picardy, France. Quiet and hard working, Colette was a big help to her mother with the housework. Her parents noticed Colette's love of prayer and her sensitive, affectionate nature.

When Colette was seventeen, both her parents died. The young woman was placed under the care of the abbot at the monastery where her father had worked. She asked for and received a hut built next to the abbey church. Colette lived there for many years. She spent her time praying and sacrificing for Jesus' Church. More and more people found out about this holy young woman. They went to see her and asked her advice about important problems. They knew that she was wise because she lived close to God. Colette received everybody with gentle kindness. After each visit, she would pray that her visitors would find peace of soul.

Colette was a member of the Third Order of St. Francis. The order of nuns started by St. Clare, who was a follower of St. Francis of Assisi, is called the Poor Clares. In 1406 St. Francis appeared to Colette. He asked her to help the Poor Clares go back to living the way he and St. Clare had taught them. Colette must have been surprised and afraid of such a difficult task. But she trusted in God's grace. Colette traveled to the Poor Clare convents. She helped the nuns become more poor and prayerful. She became a Poor Clare herself and was appointed superior of all the convents she reformed.

The Poor Clares were inspired by St. Colette's life. She had a great devotion to Jesus in the Eucharist. She also spent much time meditating on the passion and death of Jesus. She loved Jesus and her religious vocation very much.

Colette knew exactly when and where she was going to die. She died in one of her convents in Ghent, Flanders, in 1447. She was sixty-seven years old. Colette was proclaimed a saint by Pope Pius VI in 1807.

St. Colette became a leader who was able to help others because she knew how to listen to God in her heart. If we take time each day to pray and to learn about the teachings of Jesus, we will give good example to others too.

St. Perpetua and St. Felicity

Perpetua and Felicity lived in Carthage, North Africa, in the third century. It was the time of the fierce persecution of Christians by Emperor Septimus Severus.

Twenty-two-year-old Perpetua was the daughter of a rich nobleman. While growing up, she had received everything she wanted. But she realized that she loved Jesus and her Christian faith more than anything the world could offer. For this she found herself a prisoner on the way to execution.

Perpetua's father, who was not a Christian, was brokenhearted at the thought of losing his beloved daughter. He tried to convince her to reject her Christian beliefs. But Perpetua answered, "Can a jar be called anything else? Neither can I call myself anything else but what I am—a Christian." This was an especially difficult decision because Perpetua knew that she would have to leave behind her husband and baby.

Felicity, Perpetua's Christian maid, had been a slave. She and Perpetua were great friends. They shared their belief in and love for Jesus. Like Perpetua, Felicity was also willing to sacrifice her life for Jesus and for her faith. She had been sent to prison with Perpetua.

Felicity was a young wife and she was expecting a baby. Her baby was born while she was in prison. The baby was adopted by a good Christian woman. Felicity was happy because now she could die a martyr.

Hand in hand, Perpetua and Felicity bravely faced martyrdom together at the public games in the amphitheater. They were charged by wild animals and then beheaded. They died around the year 203.

The martyrs were so faithful to Jesus that they made great sacrifices. They even gave up their lives for him. Let's ask St. Perpetua and St. Felicity to help us accept cheerfully the little sacrifices that come our way.

March 8

St. John of God

John was born in Portugal on March 8, 1495. His parents were poor, but deeply Christian. As a young man, John became a soldier. He fought in the wars between France and Spain, and in Hungary. During these years he fell away, little by little, from the practice of his faith. Following his time as a soldier, John became a shepherd near Seville, Spain.

By age forty, John began to regret the way he had lived his life. He opened a shop in Granada where he sold holy pictures and religious books. At about this time, he happened to hear a sermon by the holy priest, St. John of Avila. The sermon made John think about the way he had been living. He was so sorry for the wrong he had done that he suffered a kind of breakdown and had to spend time in the hospital. St. John of Avila visited him and helped him to form a new plan for his life. After coming out of the hospital in 1539, John began to live differently. He put prayer and penance into his daily schedule. He devoted himself to helping the poor and the sick. He opened a hospital, and other men came to help him in his work. This was the beginning of the Order of Brothers Hospitalers.

It is believed that a bishop gave John his name because he changed his selfish life completely and really became a man "of God."

Some people wondered if John was as holy as he seemed. Once, a nobleman disguised himself as a beggar. He knocked on John's door, asking for a donation. John cheerfully gave him everything he had, which amounted to a few dollars. The man did not reveal his identity at the time but went away very impressed. The next day he sent a messenger to return the borrowed money to John. The messenger also brought a letter of explanation and a large sum of money. Besides making this donation, the nobleman also had fresh bread, meat and eggs—enough for all the patients and staff—

delivered every morning to the hospital that John had started.

After ten years of hard work in his hospital, John became sick himself. He died on his birthday in 1550. John of God was proclaimed a saint by Pope Innocent XI in 1690. He is the patron of the sick, nurses, and hospitals.

St. John of God listened to the advice of St. John of Avila and other spiritual people. They helped him make the right choices. It's a very good idea to ask the advice of people we trust.

March 9

St. Frances of Rome

St. Frances was born in Rome in 1384. Her parents were wealthy, but they taught Frances to be concerned about people and to live a good Christian life. She was an intelligent little girl. When she was eleven, Frances informed her parents that she had made up her mind to become a nun. Her parents encouraged her to think of marriage instead. As was the custom, they selected a good young man to be Frances's husband. The bride was just thirteen. (This was not unusual in those days.)

Frances and her husband, Lorenzo Ponziano, fell in love with each other. Even though their marriage had been arranged, they were happily married for forty years. Frances and her sister-in-law, Vannozza, prayed every day and performed penances for Jesus' Church, which had many trials at that time. Frances and Vannozza also visited the poor. They took care of the sick. They brought food and firewood to people who needed it. Other wealthy women were inspired to help the poor by their good example. When the city was struck by a plague and famine, Frances sold her jewelry in order to help the victims. Frances led a holy life of prayer, penance, and devotion to her husband and children. She was an example for her whole household, and treated her hired help as her own brothers and sisters.

Frances and Lorenzo were compassionate people. They knew what it was like to suffer. They lost two of their three children who caught the plague. This made them even more sensitive to the needs of the poor and suffering. During the wars between the real pope and the men who were claiming to be pope, Lorenzo led the armies that defended the true pope. While he was away at battle, his enemies destroyed his property and possessions. Even then, Frances cleaned up a part of the family villa that had been damaged and used it for a hospital. As hard as things were for her family, the people out on the street were in greater need.

At this time, Frances also formed a society of women living in the world without vows, dedicated to helping the poor. They were called the Oblates of Mary. Lorenzo was wounded and came home to be

Saint Dominic Savio

nursed back to health by his loving wife. After his death in 1436, Frances entered the community she had founded and became its superior.

Frances died on March 9, 1440. She was declared a saint by Pope Paul V in 1608.

St. Frances really loved Jesus and his Church. She knew that the best way to show that love was to pray for the Church. Other ways were to take good care of her family and to look after the poor. We can ask St. Frances to help us know how to show our love for Jesus and his Church.

March 10

St. Dominic Savio

Dominic Savio was born in northern Italy in 1842. One day when he was just four years old, he disappeared. When his mother went to look for him, she found Dominic kneeling in a quiet corner praying. At five, Dominic became an altar boy. When he was seven, he received his First Holy Communion. On that day, Dominic chose a motto for himself. He promised Jesus in his heart, "I will die, but I won't sin!" And he prayed every day to be true to his promise.

When he was twelve, Dominic went to the school run by St. John Bosco in Turin, Italy. Dominic missed his family, but he was happy to be at Don Bosco's school. Here he would learn everything that he would need to become a priest, which is what he wanted to do with all his heart. Dominic was a good student, but he was a lot of fun to be with, too. He was the kind of person Don Bosco and the students knew they could depend on.

Once Dominic broke up a fight between two angry boys. He held up a little crucifix and reminded the boys that they should forgive as Jesus did. Another time, Dominic noticed a group of bigger boys huddled in a circle. He worked his way through to see what was so interesting and found pornographic magazines. He grabbed them and ripped them up. The boys had never seen Dominic so angry. "Oh, what's so wrong with looking at these pictures anyway?" one of the boys blurted. "If you don't see anything wrong," Dominic said sadly, "that's even worse. It means you're used to looking at impure things!"

Sometime later, Dominic began to feel sick. He was sent home to his family to get better. But even in his hometown, his health did not improve. He grew worse instead and received the last sacraments. He began to realize that he would not be going back to Don Bosco's school. His great hope of becoming a priest was not to be fulfilled. Just before he died, Dominic tried to sit up. He said to his father, "I am seeing wonderful things." Then he rested his head on the pillow and closed his eyes. Dominic died in 1857, just a few weeks before his fifteenth birthday.

We can imitate St. Dominic Savio by asking our-selves, "Is this pleasing to God?" whenever we have to make a decision or a choice. This question will help us to make good choices.

March 11

St. Gemma Galgani

Gemma was born in Tuscany, Italy, in 1878. Her parents, Henry and Aurelia, were devout Catholics. Gemma was very close to her mother, who took time each day to pray with her and teach her about God. But Mrs. Galgani was very ill because she had caught tuberculosis when Gemma was only three. After five years of heroic suffering, Gemma's mother died. Gemma longed for someone to pray with her and talk to her about holy things as her mother had done, but no one else in the family seemed to understand her needs.

Gemma did well in school, and was liked by all her classmates and teachers. She helped out as much as she could at home, and she brought food and money to the poor. She also went to daily Mass and spent time every day praying.

When she was about nineteen, Gemma became very sick. For two years she had to stay in bed and seemed very close to death. But then St. Gabriel Possenti, a saint of the Passionist Order, appeared to her in a vision, and she was miraculously cured. After that, Gemma wanted to become a Passionist nun. But the nuns did not accept her, probably because of her weak health.

In the meantime, Gemma had been experiencing extraordinary things. She received the *stigmata*, or the five wounds of Jesus, and Jesus let her share every week in the sufferings he went through before his death. Jesus often visited Gemma. He also gave her the gift of being able to always see her guardian angel by her side.

In the spring of 1902, Gemma became sick again with tuberculosis. For a year, she grew worse and worse. She was happy to be able to share in the sufferings of Jesus, and she offered her pain to God to make up for the sins of the whole world. Gemma died on Holy Saturday, April 11, 1903. She was twenty-five years old.

Everyone experiences sadness and difficulties sometimes. Like St. Gemma, we can offer our sorrows and sufferings to God. If we do this, God will help us to feel better, and he will make us grow stronger.

March 12

Blessed Aniela Salawa

Aniela was born on September 9, 1881, near Krakow, Poland. When she was sixteen, she got a job as a housekeeper. Two years later, her sister died, and

Aniela began to think seriously about what she wanted to do with her life. She decided to dedicate herself to God.

Aniela devoted herself to prayer, and encouraged other servants to live a life of faith and prayer. Even so, she never neglected to do any of the duties given her by her employers.

In 1911, her mother, and then the woman she worked for, both died. A year later, Aniela became a member of the Franciscan Third Order. When World War I broke out, she spent her free time bringing relief and hope to the wounded in the hospitals of Krakow.

Aniela became very sick in 1917. She could no longer work, or bring comfort to others. For five years, she suffered patiently, offering her pain to God in atonement for sins and praying that those who were far away from God would turn back to him. She died on March 12, 1922 at the age of forty. She was beatified by Pope John Paul II on August 13, 1991.

Blessed Aniela shows us how to be open to the Holy Spirit. Let's allow God to work in our lives, beginning here and now, by helping those around us.

March 13

St. Seraphina (Fina)

Seraphina was born in a little Italian town called San Geminiano, near Tuscany. Her parents had once been well off, but misfortune had left them poor. Seraphina, or Fina, as her family called her, was pretty and lively. She had a generous nature. Each day she saved half of her dinner for someone in the town who was poorer than she was. During the day she sewed and spun cloth to help pay the family debts. At night, she usually spent a long time praying to Jesus and Mary.

When she was still quite young, her father died. Fina was struck with an illness that deformed and paralyzed her. It became almost impossible for her to move and she lay for six years on wooden planks. She was always in great pain and the only way she could bear it was to concentrate on Jesus as he was nailed to the cross. "I unite my sufferings to yours, Jesus," she would whisper.

Fina was left alone for many hours every day because her mother had to go out to work or beg. Then, unexpectedly, Fina's mother passed away. Now the girl was left alone. Only one neighbor, her good friend Beldia, came to care for her. Beldia tried to give Fina as much attention as she could, but she could not stay with her day and night.

It soon became clear that Fina could not live much longer. She refused to feel sorry for herself. Someone mentioned to her about the great sufferings St. Gregory the Great had gone through. Fina became devoted to him. It is said that one day, as she groaned in pain, St. Gregory appeared to her. He said kindly, "Child, on my feast day God will grant you rest." His feast day in those days was celebrated on

March 12, because he had died on March 12, 604. On March 12, 1253, St. Gregory came to take Fina home to heaven.

St. Fina helps us appreciate the Christian meaning and value of suffering. Her story also shows us how important it is for us to visit shut-ins, elderly persons, and those who are sick. We can ask St. Fina to give us a sensitive heart for people who are lonely or suffering.

March 14

St. Matilda

Matilda was born about 895. She was the daughter of a German count. When she was still quite young, her parents arranged her marriage to a nobleman named Henry. Soon after their marriage, Henry became king of Germany.

As queen, Matilda lived a simple lifestyle with times for daily prayer. Everyone who saw her realized how good and kind she was. She was more like a mother than a queen. She loved to visit and comfort the sick. She helped prisoners. Matilda did not let herself be spoiled by her position, but tried to reach out to people in need. King Henry realized that his wife was a special person. He told her many times that he was a better person and a better king because she was his wife. Even though their marriage had been arranged, Henry and Matilda really loved each other.

Matilda was free to use the treasures of the kingdom for her charities and Henry never questioned her. In fact, he became more aware of the needs of people. He realized that he had the power to ease suffering because of his position. The couple was happily married for twenty-three years. Then King Henry died quite suddenly in 936. The queen suffered the loss very much. She decided then and there to live for God alone. So she called the priest to celebrate Mass for King Henry's soul. Then she gave the priest all the jewels she was wearing. She did this to show that she meant to give up the things of the world from then on.

After years spent in practicing charity and penance, and in building three convents and a monastery, St. Matilda died peacefully in 968. She was buried beside her husband.

From St. Matilda we can learn to use whatever we have to help others less fortunate than ourselves.

March 15

St. Zachary

Zachary was born in San Severino, Italy, to a Greek family. He became a deacon in Rome, and then, in 741, pope. In his time, there was fighting all over Italy.

Pope Zachary kept making peace and saving people from terrible wars. At times he risked his life to do it.

It was because this pope was so gentle and kind that the leaders did what he asked. Zachary would do favors even for his enemies, and he gave them the kindest treatment possible. He never took revenge on them. When Pope Zachary learned that the Lombards were about to attack Rome, he asked to have a meeting with their leader. The pope and Liutprand of the Lombards met. Whatever they said to each other, the results were impressive. Liutprand canceled his attack. He also returned all the land he had taken in that area over the previous thirty years. He even released all prisoners. Liutprand signed a twenty-year treaty in which the Romans would be guaranteed freedom from attacks from the Lombards.

Pope Zachary was also known as a real father toward the poor. He built homes for the poor and for travelers. His loving heart could not bear to see people suffer. Once he heard that some businessmen had bought poor slaves in Rome and were going to sell them in Africa. He called those men and scolded them for being so cruel. Then he paid them the price they were asking for the slaves and set the slaves free.

When Zachary died in 752, all the people were saddened to have lost such a good and saintly father.

St. Zachary was a peacemaker because he was willing to talk to people who disagreed with him. Let's try to be like St. Zachary and settle arguments by listening to others. We may find that they are more open to our ideas if they know we are treating them with respect.

March 16

Blessed Torello

Torello was born around 1202, in Poppi, Italy. He grew up like all the other children of his village. But after his father's death, Torello started to change his whole way of life. He got involved with companions who drank. They hung around town all day instead of working. Torello liked his new friends and was trying hard to win their approval.

Then while he was playing an outdoor sport one day, a rooster flew down from its roost. It landed on Torello's arm and crowed three times, long and loud. Torello was speechless. He walked away and wouldn't finish the game. He couldn't help but think that what the rooster had done was no coincidence. He was being warned, just as St. Peter had once been warned, not to deny Jesus. Torello realized that the way he was living was leading him away from Jesus.

Torello decided then and there to change his life. He went to see the abbot of San Fedele, who helped him make a good confession. Then Torello went out to a quiet, wooded area and selected a spot near a big tree. He spent eight days in prayer. At the end of that time he decided that he would be a hermit. He went back to Poppi and sold all his property. He kept only enough money to buy the small square plot of land around the big tree he had found in the woods. Next to that tree he built a shack where he spent the rest of his life. He grew his own vegetables for food and got water from the stream. He led a life of prayer and penance.

Torello felt that being a hermit was what God wanted of him. This is how he peacefully spent his life. While he was alive, very few people knew of his hermit's life. Only one friend was aware of Torello's hidden life in the forest. Torello died in 1282 at the age of eighty after spending over fifty years as a hermit.

Blessed Torello realized that the way he had been living was not right. We should always try to remember that God has created us to be happy with him in heaven. If we think about this, it will help us to live in a way that pleases God.

March 17

St. Patrick

It is believed that St. Patrick was born in fifth century Britain to Roman parents. When he was sixteen, he was captured by pirates and taken to Ireland. There he was sold as a slave. His owner sent him to tend his flocks of sheep on the mountains. Patrick had very lit-

tle food and clothing. Yet he took good care of the animals in rain, snow and ice. Patrick was so lonely on the hillside that he turned often in prayer to Jesus and his mother Mary. His life was hard and unfair. But Patrick's trust in God grew stronger all the time.

Six years later, when he escaped from Ireland, Patrick decided to become a priest. After years of study and preparation, he was ordained. After some time he was made a bishop. Now what Patrick wanted more than anything else was to return to Ireland and bring the light of faith in Jesus to the Irish people. It was while St. Celestine I was pope that Patrick went back to Ireland. How happy he was to bring the Good News of the true God to the people who once had held him a slave!

Right from the start, Patrick suffered much. His relatives and friends wanted him to quit before the people of Ireland killed him. Yet Patrick kept on preaching about Jesus. He traveled from one village to another. He seldom rested, and he performed great penances for those people whom he loved so much. Before he died, the whole nation of Ireland was Christian. In spite of his great success, St. Patrick never grew proud. He called himself a poor sinner and gave all the praises to God. In his *Confessio,* Patrick wrote about his work of spreading the faith among the Irish. Most of what we know about his life comes from this writing. Patrick died in 461.

Many missionaries are working today to bring the Good News to our world just as St. Patrick did. We

can pray and make sacrifices so that their hard work
will lead many people to know and love Jesus.

March 18

St. Cyril of Jerusalem

Cyril was born around 315 when a new phase was beginning for Christians. Before that date, the Church was persecuted by the emperors. Thousands of Christians had been martyrs. In 313, Emperor Constantine recognized Christianity as a legal religion. That was a wonderful thing, but it didn't end all the problems. In fact, during the years that followed Constantine's Edict of 313, a whole new difficulty arose. There was confusion about some Christian beliefs. Some priests and bishops became brave defenders of Church teaching. One such bishop was Cyril of Jerusalem.

When St. Maximus, bishop of Jerusalem, died, Cyril was chosen to take his place. Cyril was the bishop of Jerusalem for thirty-five years. At the time, certain priests and bishops who were trying to explain the Holy Trinity became confused. A group of them, called Arians, began to teach that Jesus Christ is not God. As bishop, Cyril explained the Church's teachings very clearly. He reminded everyone that *each* of the three Persons of the Holy Trinity is God. Because Bishop Cyril disagreed with the Arians, they had him banished from Jerusalem three times. But Cyril continued to teach the truth. In 379, the Council of Antioch investigated the case and found that Cyril was teaching the correct faith.

The reign of Emperor Julian the apostate began in 361. (An apostate is someone who gives up the Christian faith.) Julian decided to rebuild the famous Temple of Jerusalem. He had a definite purpose in mind: he wanted to prove that Jesus had been wrong when he declared that the Temple of Jerusalem would not be rebuilt. So Julian spent a lot of money and sent all the materials for a new Temple. Many people helped by giving jewels and precious metals. St. Cyril calmly responded to Emperor Julian's act of pride. He was sure that the Temple could not be built, because Jesus, who is God, had said so. The bishop simply looked at all the building materials and said, "I know that this will fail." And sure enough, first a storm, then an earthquake, then a fire stopped the emperor! He finally abandoned the project.

St. Cyril died in 386 when he was around seventy. This gentle, kindly man had lived in times of upheaval and sadness. But he never lost his courage because it came from Jesus. He was faithful to the Lord all his life. Because he was so successful in explaining the truth about Christ and about his Church in difficult times, Pope Leo XIII declared St. Cyril of Jerusalem a Doctor of the Church in 1882.

St. Cyril teaches us how important it is to have a correct understanding of our Catholic faith.

Learning the teachings of Jesus and of his Church is not only for children. As we grow older and are able to understand more, we should continue to study our faith more deeply.

March 19

St. Joseph, Husband of Mary

Joseph was a good Jewish man in the family line of the great King David. His family was originally from Bethlehem in Judea, but Joseph himself was a poor carpenter living in Nazareth. Joseph was Mary's husband and Jesus' foster father. It was his great privilege and joy to take care of God's own Son, Jesus, and his mother, Mary. Joseph was happy to work for his little family. He loved Jesus and Mary very much.

Whatever the Lord wanted him to do, St. Joseph did at once, no matter how difficult it was. He was humble and pure, gentle and wise. Jesus and Mary loved him and obeyed him because God had placed him as the head of their family.

Joseph is not mentioned in the Gospel once Jesus began his ministry. This is probably because he had died by this time. We can imagine what a beautiful death St. Joseph experienced, with Mary and Jesus there beside him. For this reason, St. Joseph is prayed to as the protector of the dying.

St. Teresa of Avila chose St. Joseph as the protector of her Carmelite Order. She had great trust in his prayers. "Every time I ask St. Joseph for something," she said, "he always obtains it for me."

Pope Pius IX proclaimed St. Joseph the patron of the Universal Church. Pope Leo XIII named him as a model for fathers of families.

Let's try to obey our parents and willingly help them with the work to be done at home, just as Jesus obeyed, loved and helped Mary and St. Joseph.

March 20

St. Cuthbert

St. Cuthbert lived in England in the seventh century. He was a poor shepherd boy who loved to play games with his friends. He was very good at them, too. One of his friends scolded him for loving to play so much. In fact, his playmate said words that didn't seem to be coming from himself. The boy said, "Cuthbert, how can you waste your time playing games when you have been chosen to be a priest and a bishop?" Cuthbert was confused and very impressed when he heard this. He wondered if he really *was* going to be a priest and a bishop.

In August, 651, fifteen-year-old Cuthbert experienced something he would never forget. He saw a totally black sky. Suddenly a bright beam of light moved across it. In the light were angels carrying a ball of fire up beyond the sky. Sometime later, Cuthbert learned that the same night of the vision, the bishop, St. Aiden, had died. Cuthbert did not know how this all involved him, but he made up his mind about his life's vocation and entered a monastery. There Cuthbert became a priest.

From one village to another, from house to house, Father Cuthbert went, on horse or on foot. He visited people bringing them the Good News of Jesus. He could speak the dialect of the peasants because he himself had once been a poor shepherd boy. Cuthbert did good everywhere and brought many people to God. He was cheerful and kind. People felt attracted to him and no one was afraid of him. He was also a prayerful, holy monk.

When Cuthbert was ordained a bishop, he worked just as hard as ever to help his people. He visited them no matter how difficult it was to travel on poor roads or in very bad weather. As he lay dying, Cuthbert urged his monks to live in peace and charity with everyone. He died peacefully in 687.

St. Cuthbert went out of his way to be kind and loving with his people. We can ask him to help us to be like him so that no one will find it hard to get along with us.

March 21

St. Serapion

Serapion lived in Egypt in the fourth century. Those were exciting times for the Church and for Serapion. As a young man, he received an impressive education in his Christian faith and in all the usual subjects taught in school. For a while, he directed the famous Christian school that taught the faith in Alexandria. Then Serapion went out into the desert and became a monk. There he met the famous hermit, St. Anthony of Egypt. Serapion tried very hard to learn from Anthony and imitate him. When he died, Anthony left Serapion one of his cloaks, which Serapion treasured for the rest of his life.

Serapion became bishop of Thumis, a city in lower Egypt. He went to a very important meeting of bishops in Sardis in 347. Serapion proved to be a very brave bishop. He loved the truths of the faith and tried to protect them from those who wanted to change Christian beliefs. He worked with St. Athanasius, another brave bishop. Both were outstanding for their courage. They tirelessly explained Church teachings with their sermons and with their writings. Most of St. Serapion's writings were lost. They were letters full of instruction about the faith and an explanation of the Psalms. His most important work, a book called the *Euchologium*, was lost for hundreds of years. It was found and published at the end of the nineteenth century.

Emperor Constantius II, who disagreed with some Catholic teachings and with St. Athanasius, sent Serapion into exile. It seems that Serapion died around the year 370 in the place where he was exiled.

St. Serapion shows us by the way he lived that being a good Christian takes courage and honesty. Sometimes people may not understand or agree with our choices. But if we want to be true to Jesus and his Church, we will have to risk being unpopular at times.

March 22

St. Deogratias

The city of Carthage in Africa was taken over by barbarian armies in 439. The conquerors were the Vandals. They arrested the bishop and priests and put them on a large, old wooden raft and set it adrift at sea. Incredible as it may seem, the bishop and his priests reached the port of Naples, Italy, and were rescued. But Carthage, the city they left behind, was without a bishop for fourteen years.

Emperor Valentinian in Rome asked Genseric, the leader of the Vandals, to permit the ordination of another bishop for Carthage. Genseric agreed, and a young priest of that city was chosen. He was both respected by the conquerors and loved by the Christians. His name in Latin was "Deogratias," which means "thanks be to God." Bishop Deogratias labored for the faith and well-being of the people of Carthage.

Then Genseric attacked Rome. He returned to Africa with hundreds of slaves—men, women and children. Whole families were kidnapped and divided up among the Vandals and Moors. Genseric allowed family members to be sold and separated from their loved ones.

Bishop Deogratias heard about the tragedy. When the slave ships docked at Carthage, he bought back as many slaves as he could. He raised the money by selling the church vessels, vestments and ornaments. He was able to free many families. He found living quarters for them. When the houses were filled up, he used two large churches for this purpose. He bought everything they needed so that the people could feel at home in their new surroundings.

Bishop Deogratias died in 457 after only three years as Carthage's bishop. He was totally worn out from his life of self-sacrifice and loving service. The people he helped would never forget him.

St. Deogratias helps us realize that we can never put a price on a human life. Each person is valuable because we are all children of God, our loving Father. Let's pray to St. Deogratias that human life will be more respected.

St. Toribio de Mogrovejo

Toribio was born in 1538 in Majorca, Spain. He became a university professor and then a famous judge. He was a fine Christian with a reputation for being honest and wise.

An unusual thing happened to Toribio, and it changed his whole life. He was asked to become the archbishop of Lima, Peru. First, he was not even a priest. Second, Peru was in South America, far away from Spain. Many people in the Church realized that Toribio had the qualities for such a trusted position. He begged to be excused from the honor. But when he learned about the miserable condition of the native people of Peru, Toribio could not refuse. He wanted to help them and to bring them the faith. Toribio was ordained a priest and set out for Peru in 1581.

As archbishop, Toribio traveled all over the country. He made his way over the snowy mountains on foot. He walked over the hot sands of the seashore. He built churches and hospitals. In 1591, he established the first seminary in the Americas. Now young men of Peru could be trained to become priests who could minister to their own people. Archbishop Toribio learned the different native languages. He wanted the people to be able to listen to homilies at Mass and go to confession in their own language. He protected the natives who were often cruelly treated by their conquerors. Toribio loved the people of Peru. He spent the rest of his life as a priest and bishop for them. He died on March 23, 1606, at the age of sixty-eight. Archbishop Toribio was proclaimed a saint by Pope Benedict XIII in 1726.

We don't want to be fooled into judging the importance of people by the amount of money they have or the expensive things they own. Each one is important because God is the Father of us all. We can ask St. Toribio to help us treat every person with respect and kindness as he did.

March 24

Blessed Diego

Blessed Diego was born on March 29, 1743, in Cadiz, Spain. He was baptized Joseph Francis. His parents loved their faith and practiced it. They were delighted when Joseph constructed an altar and decorated it. He liked to kneel in front of it and pray to Jesus, to the Blessed Mother and to St. Joseph.

When he was old enough, Joseph learned how to serve Mass at the Capuchin Franciscan church just down the street. Joseph loved to go to Mass. He used to get up early enough to be at the church each morning to wait for the doors to be unlocked. He never missed a day. One of the Capuchins gave Joseph a book about the lives of the Capuchin saints. He read it and read it again. Joseph learned every story. He grew to love these holy men who were poor and humble like Jesus. The day came when he asked to join the Capuchin Order. He was accepted and went to Seville, Spain, for his novitiate training. He began a new life with a new name, Brother Diego.

After years of preparation, Brother Diego was ordained a priest. He was sent out to preach the Good News of Jesus to the people. He loved doing this. His homilies were so clear and kind that people listened. They even brought their friends to listen. Soon an ordinary church was too small for the crowds. When Father Diego was preaching, the talks were held outdoors, usually in the town square or in the streets. Father Diego loved to preach about the Holy Trinity. He was always available to hear confessions, too. He was happy when people came to the sacrament of Reconciliation. Whenever he had some free time, he visited prisons and hospitals. He also would go to visit shut-ins in their homes.

Father Diego died in 1801 and was declared "blessed" by Pope Leo XIII in 1894.

Blessed Diego lived a wonderful life for God's people. Let's ask him to help us make the most of the good influences in our lives. Such influences can be holy people, religious instruction, the Mass, and good media.

Annunciation of the Lord

Nine months before Christmas, we celebrate the moment in which our Lord Jesus Christ became man and began to grow as a baby in Mary's womb. We read about the Annunciation (the announcement of the coming of Jesus) in the Gospel of Luke (1:26-38).

When the time had arrived for God's Son to come down to us from heaven, God sent the Archangel Gabriel to the town of Nazareth where Mary lived. The archangel entered Mary's little house and said, "Hail Mary, full of grace! The Lord is with you, and you are blessed among women." Mary was surprised to hear the angel's words of praise.

"Do not be afraid, Mary," continued Gabriel. Then he told Mary that she was to be the mother of Jesus, the Son of God and our Savior.

Mary understood what a great honor God was giving her. She answered, "I am the handmaid of the Lord!" Mary knew, too, that as the mother of Jesus, she would have many sorrows. She knew she would have to suffer when her Son suffered. But with all her heart, she said, "Let everything happen as you have said." At that very moment, Mary became the Mother of God.

At the Annunciation our Blessed Mother gave us a wonderful example of humility and obedience.

Let's show God our love by obeying those who repre-sent him—our parents or guardians and teachers.

March 26

St. Margaret Clitherow

Margaret was born in York, England, in the middle of the sixteenth century. Her father was a rich candle maker. In 1571, she married John Clitherow, a well off butcher. About two or three years later, Margaret embraced the Catholic faith.

There were laws in England at the time that forbade people to be Catholics. John Clitherow was fined many times because his wife was not attending Protestant services. Because she continued to practice her Catholic faith, Margaret was put into prison for two years. As soon as she was released, she began a Catholic school for children. She rented a house where the Mass could be celebrated in secret. Catholic priests had been forced into hiding, and Margaret's home became one of their most important hiding places.

In 1584 Margaret was put under house arrest in her own home for eighteen months because she had sent her oldest son to France to receive a Catholic education. A short time later, her house was searched and a hiding place was found, containing books and articles used for Mass. Margaret was arrested and charged with hiding Catholic priests. Since this was a capital offense, she was sentenced to die on March 25, 1586. Pope Paul VI canonized brave Margaret Clitherow in 1970 as one of the Forty Martyrs of England and Wales.

It's not always easy for us to stand up for what our religion teaches us. We may worry about what others will think of us. When this happens we can pray to St. Margaret for the courage to be true to our faith in everyday life. We may even find that others are grateful for our example of faith!

March 27

St. John of Egypt

A man who desired to be alone with God was to become one of the most famous hermits of his time. St. John of Egypt was born around 304. Not much is known about his childhood except that he learned the carpenter's trade. When he was twenty-five, John decided to leave the world for good to spend his life in prayer and sacrifice for God. He became one of the famous desert hermits of that time.

For ten years he was the disciple of an elderly hermit. This holy man taught him all about the spiritual life. John called him his "spiritual father." After the older monk's death, John spent four or five years in various monasteries. He wanted to become familiar with the way monks pray and live. Finally, John found a cave high in the rocks. The area was quiet and protected from the desert sun and winds. He divided the cave into three parts: a living room, a workroom and a little chapel. People in the area brought him food and other necessities. Many also came to seek his advice about important matters. Even Emperor Theodosius asked his advice twice, in 388 and in 392.

Such well-known saints as Augustine and Jerome wrote about the holiness of St. John. When so many people came to visit him, some men became his disciples. They stayed in the area and built a hospice, a place where travelers could stay. They took care of the hospice so that more people could come to benefit from the wisdom of this hermit. St. John was able to prophesy future events. He could read the thoughts of those who came to see him. When he applied blessed oil on those who had a physical illness, they were often cured.

Even when John became famous, he kept humble and led a strict life. He died peacefully in 394 at the age of ninety.

We can ask St. John to show us how to keep close to God. St. John will help us make a real effort to put God first in our lives so that he will be able to work in and through us.

St. Tutilo

Tutilo lived in the late ninth and early tenth centuries. He was educated at the Benedictine Monastery of St. Gall in Switzerland. Two of his classmates have been declared "blessed." All three gradually became monks in the monastery where they had gone to school.

Tutilo was a person of many talents. He was a poet, a portrait painter, a sculptor, an orator, a metalworker and an architect.

His greatest talent was music. He could play all the instruments known to the monks for their liturgies. Tutilo and his friend, Blessed Notker, composed tunes for the liturgy responses. Only three poems and one hymn remain of all Tutilo's works. But his paintings and sculptures are still found today in several cities of Europe. The paintings and sculptures are identified with St. Tutilo because he always marked his works with a motto. But Tutilo was not proclaimed a saint because of his many talents. He was a humble person who wanted to live for God. He praised God the way he knew how: by painting, sculpting and composing music. Tutilo was proclaimed a saint because he spent his life praising and loving God. St. Tutilo died in 915.

Whether we have many talents or few, it's important to remember that they are gifts from God. We should develop our talents and use them to do good, just as St. Tutilo did. In this way, we'll show God that we're grateful for the gifts he has given us.

March 29

St. Jonas and St. Barachisius

King Sapor II of Persia reigned in the fourth century. He hated Christians and persecuted them cruelly. He destroyed their churches and monasteries.

Two monks named Jonas and Barachisius heard of the persecutions. They learned that many Christians had been put to death. They decided to go to help the Christians and to encourage them to remain faithful to Jesus. Jonas and Barachisius knew that they, too, might be captured. But that did not stop them. Their hearts were too full of love of others to have room for worry about their own safety.

At last the two monks were taken prisoner. They were told that if they did not worship the sun, the moon, and fire and water, they would be tortured and put to death. Of course, they refused to worship anything or anyone except the one true God. They had to suffer greatly, but they prayed. They kept thinking of how Jesus had suffered for them. The two monks endured terrible tortures but would not give up their faith. They were finally condemned to death and joyfully gave up their lives for Jesus.

Jonas and Barachisius were martyred in 327.

When we have some little pain, we can ask St. Jonas and St. Barachisius to help us offer it to Jesus. They will show us how to be brave and cheerful.

March 30

St. John Climacus

It is believed that John was born in Palestine in the sixth century. He seems to have been a disciple of St. Gregory Nazianzen. He could have become a famous teacher, but he decided to serve God with his whole heart. John joined a monastery on Mount Sinai when he was sixteen. Then he went to live for forty years by himself. He spent all his time praying and reading the lives of the saints.

At first, John was tempted by the devil. But he put all his trust in Jesus and prayed harder than ever. So the temptations never made him fall into sin. In fact, he only grew holier. He became so close to God that many heard of his holiness. They came to ask him for advice.

God gave St. John a wonderful gift. He was able to bring peace to people who were upset and tempted. Once a man who was having terrible temptations came to him. He asked St. John to help him. After they had prayed together, peace filled the poor man's soul. He was never again troubled with those temptations.

When the saint was in his seventies, he was chosen abbot of Mount Sinai. He became the superior of all the monks and hermits in the country. Another abbot asked St. John to write the rules which he had lived by all his life. This way the monks could follow his example. With great humility, St. John wrote the book called *The Ladder of Perfection,* or *The Climax of Perfection.* And that is why he is called "Climacus." St. John died in 649.

It is very wise to keep a good book in our room. We can read from it a little bit each day or before we go to bed. Reading about the lives of the saints is what helped St. John become a saint himself.

March 31

St. Guy of Pomposa

Guy lived in Ravenna, Italy, in the eleventh century. As a young man, he gave everything he owned to the poor and became a monk in Rome. He lived for three years beside the Po River with a hermit named Martin. After this he joined the monks at

Pomposa Abbey. His wisdom and holiness became well known, and soon crowds of people were flocking to see him.

The archbishop of Ravenna was considering closing the monastery, but changed his mind after meeting with Guy. In fact, because Guy was attracting so many disciples, another monastery had to be built! In his old age, Guy returned to a hermit's life. He died at Borgo San Donnino in 1046, on his way to a meeting with Emperor Henry III, who needed his advice.

When we take time each day to be close to God in prayer, we find the help we need to be like St. Guy and reach out to others who are struggling with problems or difficulties.

APRIL

April 1

St. Hugh of Grenoble

St. Hugh was born in 1052 in France. He grew up to be tall and handsome, gentle and courteous. Although he always wanted to live for God as a monk, he was given important positions instead. He was ordained a priest and then a bishop.

As bishop, Hugh began at once to correct unjust customs of some people in his diocese. He made wise plans, but that was not all he did. To draw God's mercy upon his people, Bishop Hugh prayed with his whole heart and offered sacrifices. In a short time, many of the people became virtuous and prayerful. Only some of the nobility continued to oppose him.

Bishop Hugh still thought about the life of a monk. It was what he truly wanted. He resigned as bishop of Grenoble and entered a monastery. At last, he was at peace. Yet it was not God's will for Hugh to be a monk. After a year, the pope sent him back to Grenoble again. Hugh obeyed. He knew it was more important to please God than to please himself.

For forty years, Bishop Hugh was sick nearly all the time. He had severe headaches and stomach problems. But he kept on working. He loved his people and there was so much to do for them.

Bishop Hugh died on April 1, 1132, two months before his eightieth birthday. He had been a generous and holy bishop for fifty-two years. In 1134, just two years after his death, Hugh was proclaimed a saint by Pope Innocent II.

Sometimes we think we know what's best for us, as St. Hugh thought it was best for him to be a monk. We may feel more comfortable doing one thing rather than another. But God may want us to do something completely different. We should pray to know God's will and then follow it. Doing the will of God is what makes us really happy.

April 2

St. Francis of Paola

Francis was born in the tiny village of Paola, Italy, on March 27, 1416. His parents were poor but humble and holy. They had prayed to St. Francis of Assisi for a son. When their baby was born, they named him after the saint.

When Francis was old enough, he went to a school taught by the Franciscan priests. When he was fifteen, he asked for and received his parents' permission to become a hermit and spend his life for God alone. After this, Francis went to live in a cave.

In 1436, two of his friends joined him. They built a monastery, and Francis wrote a rule of life stressing charity, humility and penance. He added a vow of fasting and abstinence from meat. In this way Francis and his community hoped to set an example for so many Christians who at that time did not take their Lenten obligations of fasting and avoiding meals of meat on certain days seriously. Francis's Order was approved by Pope Sixtus IV in 1474. They were called the Minim Friars, meaning "the littlest ones." This name was chosen because of the importance of the virtue of humility for Francis and his friars.

Everyone loved Francis. He prayed for them and worked many miracles. He told his followers that they must be kind and humble. He himself was the best example of the virtues he preached.

When King Louis XI of France was on his deathbed, he asked the pope to send Francis to him. Francis was such a source of hope and comfort for the dying king, that the king's son, Charles VIII, became Francis's lifelong friend and benefactor. Charles built a monastery in Plessis, France, for the Minims, and this is where Francis spent the rest of his life.

Francis of Paola died on Good Friday, April 2, 1507 at the age of ninety-one. He was canonized a saint in 1519.

St. Francis knew that it's very important while we're living on this earth to get ready for the life we want to spend with God forever in heaven. Sometimes we can get so wrapped up in music, television shows, videos and computer games that we forget all about God. Saying our prayers every morning when we get up and every night when we go to bed are two important ways to keep close to God.

April 3

St. Richard de Wyche

St. Richard was born in England in 1197. He and his brother became orphans when Richard was very young. His brother owned some farms. Richard gave up his studies to help him save the farms from going to ruin. He worked so hard that his grateful brother wanted to give the farms to him, but Richard would not accept them. He wanted to go away to college to get a good education. He knew that because he had very little money, he would have to work hard to pay his tuition.

Richard went to Oxford University. He was eventually given an important position at the university. Later, St. Edmund, who was archbishop of Canterbury, gave him responsible assignments in his diocese. When St. Edmund died, Richard attended the Dominican House of Studies in France. There he was ordained a priest. Then he was made the bishop of

Chichester, England, and that is why he is also known as Richard of Chichester.

King Henry III wanted someone else to be bishop. He had a friend in mind, but this person did not have the qualifications. The matter was brought to the pope in Rome and in 1245, Pope Innocent IV ruled that Richard was the valid bishop of Chichester. King Henry III was angry and refused to let Richard into his own cathedral. The king also threatened the people of Chichester with punishment if they offered Richard hospitality. But some brave people, like Father Simon, a priest from Chichester, helped Bishop Richard anyway. The two men became great friends. King Henry only gave in when the pope threatened to excommunicate him if he continued to interfere.

As bishop, Richard did his duties well. He was always gentle and kind with the people. Once in a while, he had to be stern. He was courageous and confronted people when they were doing wrong and were not sorry.

It is said that when Bishop Richard became ill, he foretold his death, because God had let him know the exact place and time when he would die. His friends, including Father Simon, were at his bedside. He died at the age of fifty-six in 1253. He was proclaimed a saint by Pope Urban IV in 1262.

As a farmer, a student, a priest and a bishop, St. Richard did his duties as well as he could. Let's ask him to help us always try our very best at home and at school.

St. Isidore of Seville

Isidore was born around the year 560 in Cartagena, Spain. His two brothers, Leander and Fulgentius, were bishops who became saints. His sister Florentina, a nun, also became a saint.

Isidore was taught by his older brother Leander. Little Isidore thought Leander was just about the meanest person in the whole world because Leander always made him study and do his homework. But the day came when Isidore realized that Leander had really been a wonderful friend. He taught Isidore that we can do so much good for Jesus' Church when we take our education seriously.

Leander became bishop of Seville, and when he died around the year 600, Isidore took his place. Isidore was bishop of Seville for thirty-seven years. He continued Leander's work of bringing the Gospel of Jesus to the Visigoths.

Isidore was an organizer, too. He was asked to direct two important Church meetings called Councils. The first was held in Seville, Spain, in 619. The second Council took place in Toledo, Spain, in 633. These Councils helped the Church become more united.

Isidore is considered one of the most learned men of his times. He understood the importance of a good education. He founded schools to train priests.

These were similar to the seminaries we have today. Isidore also wrote many works on theology, astronomy, geography, and history, as well as some biographies. Besides Spanish, he could speak and write in Latin, Greek, and Hebrew.

Isidore led a strict life and shared what he had with the poor. There was a constant stream of people at his door from morning till night. They came from all over the country because they knew he would help them.

Isidore died on April 4, 636. He was canonized in 1598. In 1722, Pope Innocent XIII declared him a Doctor of the Church.

The story of St. Isidore reminds us that our minds are a special gift from God. And it's a gift that we don't want to waste. We can ask St. Isidore to help us apply our minds to things that are really worthwhile.

April 5

St. Vincent Ferrer

Vincent Ferrer was a wonderful Christian hero. He was born in Valencia, Spain, in 1350. He had a special devotion to the Blessed Mother and was happy whenever anyone spoke of her. When he was seventeen, Vincent entered the Dominican Order, also called the Order of Preachers. He was very intelligent and did well in his studies. He was handsome too, but he wasn't proud or boastful.

From the age of twenty-one, Father Vincent taught at different colleges. Then in 1398, while he was recovering from a serious illness, Jesus appeared to him in a vision with St. Dominic and St. Francis and told Vincent to preach. For twenty years, Father Vincent preached all over Spain and France. Although there were no microphones in those days, his voice could be heard from a great distance.

Many people were touched by his words. They were so impressed by Vincent's sermons and example of holiness that they became more fervent. Catholics who were not practicing their faith often changed and began to live lives of fervor.

Vincent counted on God. He also asked people to pray and offer God sacrifices for the success of his sermons. Vincent knew that it was not his words or his talents that won people over. That is why he prayed before every sermon. But it is said that one time, when he knew that a very important person was going to listen to him, he worked harder than usual on his sermon. He ran out of time to pray. This sermon, which he had prepared so carefully, did not affect the nobleman much at all. God let that happen to teach Vincent not to count on himself. Another time, the same important person came to listen to Father Vincent preach. But this time the priest did not know it. He prayed and counted on God as usual. The nobleman listened to the sermon and was greatly touched by what he heard. When Vincent was told about it, he said, "In the first sermon it was Vincent who preached. In the second sermon, it was Jesus Christ."

Vincent died in 1419. He was proclaimed a saint by Pope Nicholas V in 1455.

Let's never brag about ourselves, or act as though we can do things on our own, without God's help. God will continue to help us all our lives if we recognize our need for him. We can ask St. Vincent to help us understand this.

April 6

Blessed Notker

This Benedictine monk, born around 840, had once been a sickly child. He had a very noticeable speech impediment all his life. But Notker was determined not to let it get in his way. This made him even more likable than he already was.

He and two other friends, Tutilo and Radpert, were very happy monks. They encouraged each other in their vocations at the monastery of St. Gall in Switzerland. Their common love for God and for music made them lifelong friends. (You can read about St. Tutilo on March 28.)

Emperor Charles visited the great monastery from time to time. He highly respected Notker and asked him for advice. Unfortunately, he didn't usually follow the advice. One time Emperor Charles sent his messenger to ask to see Notker. Notker was taking care of his garden. He sent the emperor this message: "Take care of your garden as I am taking care of mine." Emperor Charles understood that he should be taking better care of his own soul and of his kingdom.

The priest who served as the emperor's personal chaplain was very educated but very conceited. He was upset because the emperor valued Notker's opinion so much. In front of everybody at court one day, he asked Notker, "Since you are so intelligent, tell me what God is doing right now." The priest smiled at the monk, thinking that he would never have an answer. Instead Notker responded quickly, "God is doing now what he has always done. He is pushing down those who are proud and is raising up the lowly." The people started laughing as the chaplain quickly left the room.

Blessed Notker spent the rest of his life in his chosen vocation. He did many little extra things to make monastery life pleasant for the monks. With his friends, Tutilo and Radpert, he created beautiful music for the worship of God. When Blessed Notker died in 912, the entire community of monks wept.

Each of us has gifts and talents. Each of us also has weak points. It doesn't make sense to just focus on those things that we can't do well and ignore the things we're good at. Let's ask Blessed Notker to help us be grateful for our talents and use them to honor God and to help our neighbor.

April 7

St. John Baptist de la Salle

John Baptist de la Salle was born in Rheims, France, on April 30, 1651. His parents were from the nobility. John was used to elegant living. But he was a prayerful boy, too. He loved Jesus and his Church. In fact, he was studying to become a priest when both his parents died.

John had to leave the seminary and go home to take care of his brothers. But while he was teaching and training them, John kept on studying too. His brothers turned out to be fine young men. When their studies were completed, John Baptist was ordained a priest.

At that time, the nobles, like Father John Baptist's family, had the chance to be well educated. But the common people remained poor and ignorant. They had no opportunity to go to school. Father John Baptist felt very sorry for the children of the poor. He decided to do something about their situation. He began to open schools for them. To provide teachers, he started a new order, the Brothers of the Christian Schools. Although Father John Baptist also taught the children himself, he spent most of his time training the teaching brothers. For them he wrote a rule of life and a book explaining the best way to teach. Father John Baptist was one of the best educators of all time. He believed in teaching in the language of the people, not in Latin, as others did. He grouped the students into classes. He stressed the importance of silence while the lesson was being taught.

After a while, the brothers opened more schools. They taught the sons of the working people and nobles, too. Many difficulties faced the new order. But Father John Baptist's constant prayer and sacrifices blessed the work. It continued to grow and spread. Father John Baptist's health was never good. His asthma and arthritis caused him constant pain. In spite of this, he would never allow himself to take on an easier lifestyle. He died on Good Friday, April 7, 1719, at the age of sixty-eight. He was proclaimed a saint by Pope Leo XIII in 1900. Pope Pius XII declared him the patron of teachers in 1950.

St. John Baptist de la Salle and his religious congregation teach us how important our education is. Do we really try to learn from all the wonderful things we're taught in school? Do we pay attention in class and do our homework? When we begin studying, we can pray to St. John Baptist to help us.

St. Julie Billiart

Marie Rose Julie Billiart was born in France in 1751. Her uncle, the village school teacher, taught her to read and write. She especially loved to study about God. In fact, when she was just seven, Julie would explain the Catholic faith to other little children. When her parents became poor, she worked hard to help support the family. She even went to harvest the crops. Yet she always found time to pray, to visit the sick, and to teach catechism.

While she was still a young woman, Julie became very ill and completely paralyzed. Although helpless, Julie offered her prayers so that many people would find eternal happiness with God. She was more united to God than ever and kept on teaching catechism from her bed. She was a very spiritual person. People came to her for advice because she helped them grow closer to Jesus and practice their faith with more love. She encouraged everyone to receive Holy Communion often. Many young women were inspired by Julie's love for God. They were willing to spend their time and money for good works. With Mother Julie as their leader, they started the Sisters of Notre Dame de Namur.

Once a priest came to preach in the town where Julie lived. He asked her to make a novena (nine days of prayer) with him for a special intention, which he would not tell her. After five days, on the feast of the Sacred Heart, he said: "Mother, if you have faith, take one step in honor of the Sacred Heart of Jesus." Mother Julie, who had been paralyzed for twenty-two years, stood up and was cured!

Julie spent the rest of her life training young women to become sisters. She watched over her congregation. She had to suffer much from those who did not understand her mission, but she always trusted God. Her favorite words were: "How good is the good God." The Lord promised her that someday her religious congregation would be very large. And that is just what happened. Julie died on April 8, 1816. Today there are many of her sisters all over the world. Mother Julie was proclaimed a saint by Pope Paul VI in 1969.

Whenever we're worried about something, let's pray, "Jesus, I trust in you." This will help us remember the goodness of God, as St. Julie always did. God never stops loving us and watching over us.

April 9

St. Madeleine Sophie Barat

Madeleine Sophie Barat was born in Burgundy, France, on December 12, 1779. Her father was a barrel maker, and she received her education from her older brother Louis. Louis was very strict, and taught Sophie to live a disciplined life. When Louis entered the seminary, he made sure that his sister had a share in what he himself was studying. Afterwards, Louis took her to Paris to continue her studies. She stayed with a good Catholic woman. With a group of other girls she studied, prayed, worked, and even taught classes for poor girls.

Sophie wanted to become a nun, but because of the French Revolution, all the convents had been closed. As years passed, the little group of young women who prayed, worked and taught together seemed more and more like a religious community. A priest named Father Varin wanted to begin a new religious order for women who would dedicate themselves to educating girls. Louis heard about this and recommended his sister. Sophie and three of her friends joyfully agreed and in 1800 they became the first sisters of the Society of the Sacred Heart of Jesus. The following year they opened their first convent and school, with Sophie, although the youngest at twenty-three, as the superior of the little community.

Mother Barat, as Sophie was now called, encouraged her sisters and students to love the Sacred Heart of Jesus. She rejoiced when there were twenty-four sisters in the community. Now they could take turns, hour by hour, to adore Jesus in the Eucharist day and night. The Society of the Sacred Heart grew, and convents and schools opened all over France. One of the sisters, Mother Rose Philippine Duchesne, who became a missionary to the United States, is also a canonized saint. (Her story is found in volume 2 of this set of books.)

Mother Barat lovingly guided her sisters for sixty-three years. She experienced many difficulties in traveling to open new schools, establish new convents, and visit her sisters. By the time she died in 1865, her order had over a hundred houses and schools in twelve different countries.

God gave St. Madeleine Sophie the gift of being very good at teaching. God has given each of us special gifts and talents too. By developing our natural abilities, we can better serve God and our neighbor.

April 10

Blessed Antoine Frédéric Ozanam

Frédéric Ozanam was born on April 23, 1813, in Milan, Italy. He was raised and educated in Lyons, France. As a teenager, he experienced a period of time when he struggled with the truths about God that he had been taught. But his teacher patiently explained these things in a way that helped young Frédéric overcome his doubts. Frédéric was always grateful to this teacher who helped him to form clear ideas about the truths he believed. All through his life, remembering this experience helped him to explain the Catholic faith to others in a spirit of understanding and kindness.

When he grew up, Frédéric went to Paris to study law. While he was there, he met many important Catholic thinkers of his time. Following their example, he dedicated himself to explaining the Catholic Church's teachings, which were under attack by some people at that time. In May of 1833, Frédéric formed a group that would later be known as the Society of St. Vincent de Paul. This society would put the teachings of Jesus into practice by helping the poor.

After practicing law in Lyons, Frédéric returned to Paris to study literature and history. He continued his activities in the Society of St. Vincent de Paul. He also wrote articles for the Catholic newspapers. Frédéric always stood up for the rights of the poor and encouraged other Catholics to do the same.

In June 1841, Frédéric married Amelie Soulacroix. They had a daughter named Marie. Frédéric was a wonderful husband and father. At the same time he continued his visits to the poor and his work for social justice. He died on September 8, 1853, in Marseilles, France. Pope John Paul II declared him blessed in 1997.

Blessed Frédéric teaches us that as true followers of Jesus we have the duty to do what we can to bring justice and charity to all members of society. Today, if we see someone being treated unfairly, let's ask Blessed Frédéric to help us be courageous in standing up for that person.

April 11

St. Stanislaus

St. Stanislaus was born near Kracow, Poland, in 1030. His parents had prayed for thirty years for a child. When Stanislaus was born, they offered him to God because they were so grateful to have him. When he grew up, Stanislaus went to study in Paris, France. After his parents died, he gave all the money and property they had left him to the poor. Then he became a priest.

In 1072, Stanislaus was made the bishop of Kracow. Bishop Stanislaus won the love of all the people. He was an excellent preacher, and many people turned to him for spiritual advice. They especially appreciated the way he took care of the poor, the widows and the orphans. Often he served them himself.

Poland's king at that time was Boleslaus II. He was cruel and was living in a sinful way. The people were disgusted with his lifestyle and were afraid of him. Bishop Stanislaus first corrected him privately. The bishop was kind and respectful. But he was honest, too, and told the king that what he was doing was wrong. The king seemed sorry, but soon fell back into his old ways. He committed even more shameful sins. The bishop then had to put him out of the Church. King Boleslaus flew into a rage at that. To get revenge, he ordered two of his guards to kill Stanislaus. Three times they tried, and three times they failed. When the king heard this, he was angrier than ever. He himself rushed into the bishop's chapel and murdered Bishop Stanislaus as he was celebrating Mass. It was April 11, 1079.

God worked many miracles after Stanislaus's death. All the people called him a martyr. He was proclaimed a saint by Pope Innocent IV in 1253. St. Stanislaus is the patron saint of Poland.

It takes courage to correct people who are hurting others and giving bad example. Sometimes we might have to be corrected for our own mistakes. Let's ask St. Stanislaus to help us correct our faults and bad habits. Let's also ask him to help us to be grateful to those who challenge us to become better.

April 12

St. Joseph Moscati

Joseph Moscati was born on July 25, 1880, in Benevento, Italy. He was the seventh of nine children. His father became a judge in Naples, so the entire family moved to that city. There was a hospital near the Moscati home. Each day, as Joseph saw

the sick and suffering patients of the hospital, he thought more and more of how he could help them. He decided to become a doctor, and enrolled in Naples University.

When he was twenty-two, Dr. Moscati began his service at the Hospital of the Incurables. Later he opened his own office. All patients were welcome whether they could pay or not. Dr. Moscati would write prescriptions for poor patients, then pay for the medicine out of his own pocket. Every day was long and hard, but Dr. Moscati remained gentle and kind. He made the effort to listen carefully to each of his patients. He encouraged them and prayed for them.

In 1906, when Mt. Vesuvius became active, Dr. Moscati risked his life to go to a hospital in the area of the volcano and evacuate the patients. The roof of the hospital fell in soon after the last patient was moved out.

Besides being an excellent doctor, Joseph Moscati was holy too. How did he do it? Each morning he went to Mass and spent time in prayer. Then the doctor would visit the sick poor in the slums of Naples. From there he would go to the hospital and begin his rounds. For twenty-five years, Joseph worked and prayed for his patients. He knew that the well-being of the soul often affected the health of the body. Along with prescriptions for medication, Dr. Moscati would prescribe prayer and a return to the sacraments, often with dramatic results! He poured all his strength into his life's calling.

On the afternoon of April 12, 1927, Dr. Moscati did not feel well, so he went to his office and relaxed in an armchair. There he had a stroke and died. He was forty-seven years old.

We can ask St. Joseph to help us be as honest, kind and sympathetic as he was. We can also ask him to teach us how to appreciate the Mass and to love Mary as he did.

April 13

St. Martin I

Martin was a priest of Rome who had a reputation for being wise and holy. He became pope in July, 649. When people were arguing over the truths about Jesus, Pope Martin held a special meeting of bishops. This meeting was called the Council of the Lateran. It explained clearly what we believe about certain truths of our faith. Some Christians were not pleased with the results of the meeting. But Pope Martin knew that the Council's explanations were true, and it was his duty as pope to teach people the truth.

Some powerful men did not appreciate Pope Martin's activities. One such person was Emperor Constans II of Constantinople. The emperor sent his soldiers to Rome to capture Martin and bring him to Constantinople. The soldiers kidnapped the pope.

They took him right out of the Lateran Cathedral and brought him onto a ship. Pope Martin got sick, but they continued their journey. In October, 653, the pope was put in jail in Constantinople for three months. He was given only a little food and water each day. He wasn't even allowed to wash himself. Pope Martin was convicted of treason without a hearing. He was publicly humiliated and condemned to death. But then he was sent back to the same prison for three more months. Patriarch Paul of Constantinople pleaded for the pope's life. So instead of death, the pope was sentenced to be exiled. Pope Martin was put on a ship that took him across the Black Sea. In April, 654, it landed on the Russian peninsula called the Crimea.

Pope Martin suffered very much while he was in prison. He wrote his own account of those sad days. The pope said that he felt very bad to be forgotten by his relatives and members of the Church in Rome. He knew that they were afraid of the emperor. But at least they could have sent him food and clothing. But they did not. They abandoned the pope out of fear.

Pope Martin's exile lasted two years. He died of neglect and ill-treatment around 656. Because of his terrible sufferings, he was proclaimed a martyr. He is the last of the popes so far to be considered a martyr.

When the Church teaches us something, we can be sure that it is true and good, even if some people disagree with it. The Church cannot teach us anything that is false because it is guided by the Holy Spirit. We want to be like St. Martin and always follow the truth.

April 14

Blessed James Duckett

James Duckett was an Englishman who lived during the reign of Queen Elizabeth I. As a young man he became an apprentice printer in London. This is how he came across a book called *The Firm Foundation of the Catholic Religion.* He studied it carefully and believed that the Catholic Church was the true Church. In those days, Catholics were persecuted in England. James decided that he wanted to be a Catholic, even if he had to face the serious consequences.

The clergyman at his former church came to look for him because James had been a steady churchgoer. But James would not go back. Twice he served short prison terms for his refusal to attend Protestant services. Both times his employer interceded and got him freed. But then the employer asked James to find a job somewhere else.

James knew there was no turning back. He sought out a disguised Catholic priest in the Gatehouse prison. The old priest, who went by the name of "Mr. Weekes," instructed him. James was received into the

Catholic Church. He married a Catholic widow and their son became a Carthusian monk. The monk is the one who wrote down much of what we know about his father.

James Duckett never forgot that it was a book that had started him on the road to the Church. He considered it his responsibility to provide his neighbors with Catholic books. He knew these books encouraged and instructed them. So dangerous was this "occupation" that he was in prison for nine out of twelve years of his married life. James was finally brought to trial and condemned to death on the testimony of one man, Peter Bullock, a bookbinder. Mr. Bullock testified that he had bound Catholic books for James Duckett, and this was a "grave offense." Mr. Bullock turned traitor because he was in prison for unrelated matters and he hoped to be freed.

Both men were condemned to die on the same day. On the scaffold at Tyburn, James Duckett assured Peter Bullock of his forgiveness. He kept encouraging the man as they were dying to accept the Catholic faith. Blessed Duckett was martyred in 1602.

The story of Blessed James shows us how powerful the media—books, television shows, movies and music—are. Reading just one good book changed his whole life. Let's ask Blessed James to help us to watch, listen to and read only what is good.

April 15

St. Anna Schäffer

This saint was born in Bavaria, Germany, in 1882. When she was old enough to help support her large family, Anna started working. She hoped that one day she would be able to enter the convent and become a missionary sister. In order to prepare herself, Anna offered her life to God and did all she could to help others in need.

When she was nineteen, Anna had a terrible accident in the laundry where she worked. She fell into a tub of boiling bleach. She spent a year in the hospital, and was treated by specialists. The doctors tried their best, but they were unable to heal her wounds. Anna was confined to her bed for the rest of her life. Because she was unable to work, she was forced to live in poverty.

At first, Anna felt angry about the way things had turned out for her. But little by little, she began to understand the value of suffering, especially when it was united to Jesus' sufferings on the cross. She realized that she could still help others, but in a different way than she had originally hoped. She could offer her sufferings to Jesus for the salvation of souls. The priest who brought Anna Holy Communion every morning noticed the change in her. At the end of her life, he could say that he never heard her complain in the twenty-five years that he knew her.

Besides offering her sufferings to God, Anna was able to use her sewing needle to embroider beautiful linens for churches. She especially liked to embroider images of Jesus' Sacred Heart. Anna also wrote letters to people in Austria, Switzerland, and America. These people wrote to her and asked for prayers and advice, and she wrote back to them with words of faith and hope and love of God. By writing these letters, Anna had become a missionary after all.

Anna Schäffer died in 1925. Pope John Paul II declared her blessed in 1999. She was canonized on October 21, 2012 by Pope Benedict XVI.

We are all called to do what we can to help others grow closer to God. Is there anyone you know who is sad or suffering? Why not do what St. Anna did and send a little note or card to cheer that person up and promise him or her your prayers.

April 16

St. Benedict Joseph Labre

This French saint, born in 1748, led a most unusual life. He was the son of a storeowner and was taught by his uncle, a priest. When the good priest died, Benedict tried to enter a monastery. But he was told that he was too young. Next Benedict contacted another order of monks. He loved their life of prayer and penance. But after he joined them, Benedict became thin and weak. The monks suggested that he return home to lead a good Christian life. Benedict went home and slowly gained back his health. He prayed for God's help. Then he felt he was given an answer. He would become a pilgrim, a person on a holy journey of prayer and penance. As a pilgrim, he would travel to the famous shrines of Europe.

Benedict began his journey on foot. He visited one church after another. He wore a plain cloth robe, a crucifix over his heart and a rosary around his neck. He slept on the bare ground. The only food he had was what kind people gave him. If they gave him money, he passed it on to the poor. His "suitcase" was a sack. In it he carried his own Gospel, as well as medals and holy books to give to others.

Benedict paid no attention to the beautiful sights in the cities he visited. His only interest was in the churches where Jesus dwelt in the Blessed Sacrament.

In 1774, Benedict stayed in Rome. People began calling him "the beggar of Rome." He never asked for anything that would make his life more comfortable. Sometimes children threw stones at him and called him names. People who didn't know him tended to avoid him. But when Benedict knelt in front of the tabernacle, he became as still as a statue. His pale, tired face glowed. He would talk to Jesus and to the

Blessed Mother. He would whisper, "Mary, O my Mother!" He was really the happiest when he was keeping Jesus and the Blessed Mother company.

Benedict died in Rome in 1783 at the age of thirty-five. The fame of this poor holy man spread far and wide. His journey had ended. His pilgrimage was over. Now he would be with Jesus and Mary forever. One hundred years after his death, Benedict Joseph Labre was proclaimed a saint by Pope Leo XIII in 1883.

Even if we can't imitate the poverty of Jesus in the way St. Benedict Joseph did, we can imitate his love for Jesus in the Holy Eucharist. Let's go to church as often as we can to visit Jesus in the Holy Eucharist and talk to him about all that is in our hearts. Jesus is the best friend we have!

April 17

St. Stephen Harding

Stephen was a young Englishman who lived in the twelfth century. He was a good student who liked to learn. Stephen was especially interested in literature. He was serious about life and prayed daily. Once Stephen and his friend set out on foot as pilgrims for Rome. When they returned, Stephen joined a very poor and holy group of monks. These men prayed, fasted and worked hard. That was their way of showing their love for God. Stephen noticed how happy they were. Their abbot was another saint, St. Robert.

For a while, Stephen served God joyfully with them. After a while, St. Robert, Stephen and twenty other monks received permission to start a new monastery. They built it themselves in a wilderness in France called Citeaux. There they lived a life of work and great poverty because they wanted to imitate the poverty of Jesus. They also kept strict silence. The monks of this new monastery were called Cistercians.

When Stephen became the abbot of the monastery, he had many troubles. His monks had only a little food. Then over half of them became sick and died. It looked as though the community would come to an end. The monks needed new, young members to continue their life. Stephen prayed with faith. And his prayer was rewarded. God sent thirty young men who wanted to join the monks. They arrived at the monastery gate all together. Their leader, Bernard, was to become a great saint, too. (We celebrate St. Bernard's feast day on August 20.) It was a wonderful day for Abbot Stephen and his monks!

Stephen spent the last few years of his life writing a book of rules for the monks. He also trained Bernard to take his place. St. Stephen Harding died in 1134.

We might not think about it much, but it's important to spend some quiet time each day lis-

tening to God who speaks in our hearts. St. Stephen knew that this is why some silence in our lives is important. We can ask him to remind us to sometimes turn off our TVs, CD players, and computers to spend time listening to and talking to God!

April 18

St. Marie of the Incarnation

Barbara was born in France in 1566. She was married to Peter Acarie, an aristocrat, when she was seventeen. She and her husband loved their Catholic faith and practiced it. The couple had six children, and their family life was happy. Barbara tried to be a good wife and mother. Her family learned from her a great love for prayer and works of charity.

Once, when her husband was unjustly accused of a crime, Barbara herself saved him. She went to court, and, all alone, proved that he was not guilty.

Although she was busy with her own family, Barbara always found time to feed those who were hungry. She instructed people in the faith. She helped the sick and dying. She gently encouraged people who were living sinfully to change their ways. The good deeds she performed were works of mercy.

When her husband died, Barbara entered the Carmelite Order. She spent the last four years of her life as a nun. Her three daughters had become

Carmelites, too. Barbara's new name as a nun was Sister Marie of the Incarnation. She joyfully worked in the kitchen among the pots and pans. When her own daughter became the superior of the monastery, Sister Marie willingly obeyed her. She wanted to be humble, as Jesus was.

St. Marie died in 1618. She was fifty-two years old. Pope Francis canonized her on April 3, 2014.

St. Marie became close to God even though her life was always very busy. She had many responsibilities. She took care of her family. She also was thoughtful about helping others. Let's ask her to help us to be responsible and generous with our lives, too.

April 19

Blessed Marcel Callo

Marcel was born in France on December 6, 1921. He was one of nine children, and his parents belonged to the working class. Marcel went to school until he was twelve. Then he went to work with a printer as an apprentice (someone who is being trained). He also joined a group called the Young Christian Workers, which gave him an opportunity to reach out and help those in need.

In 1942 Marcel was just beginning to make plans to get married when the Nazis moved into France and took over. Marcel, the leader of the Young Christian Workers, organized his friends and together they helped many people escape. The Nazis then forced him to go to Germany to work in a weapons factory. Full of faith and hope, Marcel saw this as a chance to help others who were having doubts about God and their faith. He started a Young Christian Workers group in the labor camp. He was arrested in 1944 for practicing his Catholic faith and for making arrangements to have a Mass celebrated. Marcel was sent from one concentration camp to another. He and his fellow prisoners were put to work building airplanes. They worked underground in terrible living conditions and they were not given enough to eat. But Marcel's faith did not weaken. He tirelessly reached out to the other prisoners with encouragement and hope.

In January of 1945, Marcel was hospitalized. Two months later he died of malnutrition and exhaustion at Mauthhausen Concentration Camp in Austria. Pope John Paul II declared him "Blessed" on October 4, 1987.

How strong is our faith and hope? When things go wrong, do we get easily discouraged? We can pray to Blessed Marcel to help us be persons of faith and hope even in difficult situations.

St. Agnes of Montepulciano

This saint was born near the city of Montepulciano, Italy, in 1268. When she was just nine years old, she begged her mother and father to let her live at the nearby Dominican convent. Agnes was very happy with the sisters. They led a quiet, prayerful life. They worked hard, too. Even though she was young, Agnes understood why the sisters lived and prayed so well. They wanted to be very close to Jesus.

When she was old enough, Agnes received her training as a novice. She was such a good nun that the other sisters were pleased to have her. Because of Agnes' example of prayer and holiness, many young women came to join the community of Dominican nuns.

When she was still quite young, Agnes was chosen superior or "prioress" of the convent. She tried to be fair and honest with each sister. She kept reminding herself that everything she did was for Jesus. She believed that Jesus was really in charge of the convent. He was taking care of them.

Mother Agnes lived a life of penance. She was kind and gentle even when she didn't feel like it. God filled Agnes with joy and sometimes gave her spiritual favors. One time he even let her hold Baby Jesus in her arms.

Agnes did not have good health. But she was patient even when she was very ill. She never complained or felt sorry for herself. Instead, she offered everything to God. Toward the end of her life, the sisters realized she was not going to get better. They were very sad. "If you loved me, you would be glad," Agnes said. "I am going to enter the glory of Jesus."

Agnes died in 1317 at the age of forty-nine. She was proclaimed a saint in 1726. Her tomb became a place of pilgrimage. Many people came to pray to this holy woman and to ask her to pray to God for them. Among the pilgrims was the famous St. Catherine of Siena. (We celebrate St. Catherine's feast day on April 29.)

The story of St. Agnes teaches us that we are never too young to begin serving God. When we love the Lord and spend each day for him, our lives become beautiful gifts that we give back to God.

April 21

St. Anselm

Anselm was born in northern Italy in 1033. From his home he could see the Alps mountains. When he was fifteen, Anselm tried to join a monastery in Italy. But his father was against it. Then Anselm became sick. Not long after he got better, his mother died. He was still young and rich and clever. Soon he forgot about wanting to serve God. He began to think only of having good times.

After a while though, Anselm became bored with this way of life. He wanted something better, something more important. He went to France to visit the holy Abbot Lanfranc of the famous monastery of Bec. Anselm became Lanfranc's very close friend and the abbot brought him closer to God. He also helped Anselm decide to become a Benedictine monk. Anselm was then twenty-seven.

Anselm was a warm-hearted man who loved his brother monks very much. He became the abbot in 1078. When he had to leave Bec to become archbishop of Canterbury in England, he told the monks that they would always live in his heart.

The people of England loved and respected Anselm. However, King William II persecuted him. Anselm had to flee into exile in 1097 and in 1103. King William even forbade Anselm to go to Rome to ask the pope's advice. But Anselm went anyway. He stayed with the pope until the king died. Then he went back to his diocese in England.

Even in the midst of his many duties, Anselm always found time to write important books of philosophy and theology. He also wrote down the many wonderful instructions he had given the monks about God. They were very happy about that. He used to say: "Would you like to know the secret of being happy in the monastery? Forget the world and be happy to forget it. The monastery is a real heaven on earth for those who live only for Jesus."

St. Anselm died on April 21,1109. He was declared a great teacher or Doctor of the Church by Pope Clement XI in 1720.

There's nothing wrong with having good, clean fun. But what we need to remember, as St. Anselm found out, is that fun is not the same as true happiness. We will only be really happy when we are spending our time doing worthwhile things for God and our neighbor.

April 22

St. Lidwina

The name Lidwina means "suffering." Lidwina was from Holland. She was born in 1380 and died in 1433. When she was fifteen, Lidwina dedicated herself completely to God. She might have become a nun some day. But in a single afternoon, her entire life was changed.

When she was sixteen, Lidwina went skating with her friends. One of them accidentally bumped into her. Lidwina fell down hard on the ice and broke a rib. This was very painful. But the fall triggered other problems, too. In the days ahead, she began to have severe headaches, and experience nausea, fever, thirst, and pain throughout her whole body.

Crying, Lidwina told her father she could not stand the pain anymore. But the pain increased. She developed sores on her face and body. She became blind in one eye. Finally, she could no longer get out of bed.

Lidwina became frustrated and bitter. Why had God let this happen to her? What did he want from her? And what could she still give to him anyway? Her parish priest, Father John, came to visit and pray with her. He helped her think of what Jesus had suffered. Lidwina began to realize the special gift that she could give to Jesus: she would suffer for him. She would offer her sufferings to console Jesus, who had suffered so much for all of us on the cross. Little by little, Lidwina's suffering became a beautiful prayer that she offered to God.

Lidwina was very sick for thirty-eight years. It seemed impossible that she could remain alive in such a serious condition. But she did. And God comforted her in many ways. Lidwina was good and kind to everyone who came to visit her poor little room. She helped her visitors by praying for them and their special intentions.

Lidwina's special love was for Jesus in the Holy Eucharist. For the last nineteen years of her life, she needed no other food except Holy Communion. This was a special gift God gave her.

St. Lidwina shows us that we can offer any physical pain to Jesus as an act of love. Her story also reminds us that we should always thank God for our health.

April 23

St. Adalbert

This saint was born in Bohemia in 956. He went to school in Magdeburg. After his teacher died, Adalbert returned to Bohemia. He was named bishop of Prague in 982. After a while, it seemed to Adalbert that his preaching and work as a bishop were not having any effect on the people of Prague, and he became discouraged. He went to Rome in 990 and became a Benedictine monk. But the Duke of Poland asked the pope to send Adalbert back to Prague, and he returned.

One day, a woman of Prague was accused of a serious sin for which the punishment was death. Bishop Adalbert let her stay in the church for protection, but a furious crowd stormed the church, dragged her out and killed her. Bishop Adalbert excommunicated (someone who is excommunicated is separated from the Church and can no longer receive the sacraments) everyone involved with the woman's murder. Because of this incident, he was forced to leave Prague once again, and went back to the Benedictine monastery in Rome.

Pope Gregory V ordered Adalbert to go back to Prague, but his enemies were ready to use violence if he returned. So Adalbert was sent instead to Pomerania, Hungary and Russia to preach the

Gospel. People mistook Bishop Adalbert and his missionary companions, Benedict and Gaudentius, for Polish spies. They were murdered in 997.

What matters to God is that we try our best to do our duty, whatever it might be. We shouldn't get discouraged if we're not successful, or if others are against us. When we love God and make an honest effort to do what is right, as St. Adalbert did, we're always a success in God's eyes.

We also celebrate the feast of St. George on this date.

April 24

St. Fidelis of Sigmaringen

This saint's name was Mark Rey. He was born in Germany in 1578. Mark went to the famous University of Freiburg to become a lawyer. Even as a student, he liked to visit the sick and the poor. He spent time praying daily. His brother chose to become a Capuchin Franciscan priest. Mark, instead, finished his studies and became a very good lawyer.

Mark often took on the cases of poor people who had no money to pay. This won him the nickname, "The Poor Man's Lawyer." Because he was very honest, Mark soon became disgusted with the dishonesty of the law courts. He decided to follow his brother and become a priest. He received his religious habit and took the new name Fidelis, which means "faithful."

Father Fidelis was filled with joy when he was assigned to Switzerland to preach the Good News. At that time in Switzerland there were many people who had left the Catholic faith. Father Fidelis wanted to win these people back to the Church. His preaching brought wonderful results. Many people were converted. But enemies of the Church grew angry at his success.

Fidelis knew that his life was in danger, yet he went right on preaching. In the middle of a sermon one day, someone fired a shot at him, but the bullet missed. Father Fidelis knew he had to leave the town at once. As he was walking down the road to the next town, a mob of angry men stopped him. They ordered him to give up the Catholic religion. "I will not give up the Catholic faith," Father Fidelis answered firmly. Then the men pounced on him and beat him with their clubs and tools.

The wounded priest pulled himself up to a kneeling position. He prayed: "Lord, forgive my enemies. They do not know what they are doing. Lord Jesus, have mercy on me! Holy Mary, my Mother, help me!" The men attacked him again until they were certain he was dead.

Fidelis died a martyr in 1622 at the age of forty-four. He was proclaimed a saint by Pope Benedict XIV in 1746.

It's a great honor to be able to help others come to know Jesus and his Church. Let's try by prayer, good example and kind words, to be real apostles in imitation of St. Fidelis.

April 25

St. Mark the Evangelist

Mark lived at the time of Jesus. Although he was not among the original twelve apostles, he was a relative of St. Barnabas the apostle. Mark is well known because he wrote one of the four Gospels. That is why he is called an "evangelist," which means "Gospel writer." Mark's Gospel is short, but it gives many little details that are not in the other Gospels.

While he was still young, Mark went with the two great saints, Paul and Barnabas, on a missionary journey to bring the teachings of Jesus to new lands. Before the journey was over, though, Mark seems to have had a disagreement with St. Paul. Mark suddenly returned to Jerusalem. Paul and Mark later worked out their differences. In fact, Paul wrote from prison in Rome that Mark came to console and help him.

Mark also became a beloved disciple of St. Peter, the first pope. St. Peter called St. Mark "my son." Some think that Peter meant to say that he had baptized Mark. Mark was consecrated a bishop and sent to Alexandria, Egypt. There he converted many people. He worked hard to spread love for Jesus and his Church. It is believed that he went through long and painful sufferings before he died around the year 74.

St. Mark's relics were brought to Venice, Italy. He is the patron saint of that famous city. People go to the beautiful basilica of St. Mark to honor him and to pray to him. In art, St. Mark's symbol is the lion.

We can remember St. Mark when we have a disagreement with someone, or when we find it hard to get along with someone. At those times, we can ask St. Mark to help us work out our disagreements in kindness and respect.

April 26

St. Zita

Zita is known as the patron saint of housekeepers. She was born in the village of Monte Sagrati, Italy, in 1218. Her parents were deeply religious and raised Zita in a loving, Christian way. In those days it was the custom of poor couples to send their teenage daughters to trustworthy families who could afford servants. The young women would live with the families for a time and were employed to do the household tasks. Zita was sent to the Fatinelli family in Lucca when she was twelve years old.

Mr. and Mrs. Fatinelli were good people who had several other employees. Zita was happy to be able to work and send money home to her parents. She formed habits of praying that fit in with her new schedule. She even got up early to go to daily Mass.

Zita was very conscientious and always did her best. To her, work was an expression of her love for God. But the other workers were annoyed. They tried to do as little as they could get away with. They began to pick on Zita and oppose her without their employers noticing. Zita was hurt, but she prayed for patience. She never told on the workers. She insisted on doing her work as well as possible no matter what the others thought of her.

After some time, Zita was made the head house-keeper. The Fatinelli children were placed under her care. Then the other workers stopped bothering her. Some of them even began to imitate her.

Zita spent her whole life with the Fatinelli family. While other workers came and went, she stayed. She loved the Fatinellis like she loved her own family and she served them well. By her example, she helped people see that work is beautiful when it is done with Christian love. Zita died peacefully on April 27, 1278. She was sixty years old.

St. Zita has a wonderful lesson for us all. She reminds us that what we do reflects the kind of person we are. Our work and our study take effort. But they're worth the trouble because God will reward us in heaven.

April 27

St. Gianna Beretta Molla

Gianna Beretta was born on October 4, 1922, near Milan, Italy. She grew up in a Christian home, and her parents carefully passed on to her their Catholic faith. As a teenager, she was active as a member of Catholic Action groups. When she was sixteen, she made up her mind that she would rather die than commit a mortal (very serious) sin, and that she wanted to do everything for Jesus.

Her parents' deaths, four months apart in 1942, were a heavy blow to Gianna, who was just beginning medical school at the University of Milan. After six semesters, she continued her preparation at the University of Pavia, where she earned a doctorate in medicine on November 30, 1949.

Gianna opened a clinic in 1950. She soon had many patients. In addition to her work as a physician, Gianna also devoted her time to community projects. She continued to be an active member of Catholic Action groups too. She organized talks and retreats, hikes and social events, and was very successful in reaching out to young people. Pietro Molla, a prosperous engineer, who belonged to one of the Catholic Action groups, was impressed with this dynamic young doctor who cared so much about others. Gianna had been planning to become a medical missionary sister in Brazil. Her brother was a priest there, and she knew he would be happy to have her help him. But once she got to know Pietro, Gianna wondered if it was God's will for her to marry him and start a family. After much prayer, she asked the advice of her confessor. The priest answered her, "If every good Catholic girl became a nun, there would be no Christian mothers!"

Pietro and Gianna were married on September 24, 1955. Gianna was thirty-three. In 1956, their first child, Pierluigi was born. Mariolina was born in 1957, and Laura came along in 1959. After that, Gianna lost two more babies before they were born. But she became pregnant again in 1961. After two months, she started to experience pain, and her doctor found a tumor in her uterus. Before undergoing the necessary surgery, Gianna gave her surgeons strict orders to keep her unborn child safe. The following April, just before the baby was to be born, Gianna told her doctor, "If you have to choose between my life and the life of the baby, I demand that you save the baby's life." As a doctor herself, Gianna was well aware of the risks she was facing, and she wanted her wishes known.

On April 21, Gianna had a healthy baby girl, who was baptized Gianna Emanuela. But Gianna was dying from complications in the delivery. She asked Pietro to take her home so she could die in her own room. There, on April 28, 1962, Doctor Gianna Beretta Molla died. Her daughter, Gianna Emanuela, who has been called the "living relic of her mother," followed in her mother's footsteps and became a doctor. On April 24, 1994, with understandable joy and pride, she was present at the beatification ceremony for her mother, who selflessly gave her own life so that she could live. Gianna was named a saint ten years later in 2004.

Jesus said, "There is no greater love than to lay down one's life for a loved one" (John 15:13). That's exactly what St. Gianna Beretta Molla did. Let's ask this brave and unselfish saint to help everyone understand the sacredness of human life.

April 28

St. Peter Chanel

Peter Chanel was born near Belley, France, in 1803. From the time he was seven, he took care of his father's sheep. Though poor, he was intelligent and loved his faith, too. One day, a good parish priest met him. He thought so much of Peter that he asked his parents if he could educate the boy. In this priest's little school, and later in the seminary, Peter studied hard. When he became a priest in 1827, he was sent to a parish where just a few Catholics still practiced their faith. Father Peter was prayerful. He was kind and patient with everyone. In just three years there was a big improvement in his parish. Many people became full of love for

Jesus and his Church again because of Father Peter's help and example.

Father Peter had a great desire to become a missionary. He joined a religious order called the Marists. He hoped he would be sent to bring the Gospel to people who did not yet know about Jesus. After a few years, his wish came true. He and a group of Marist missionaries were sent to the islands of the South Pacific. Father Peter and one brother were assigned to the island of Futuna. There the people willingly listened to Father Peter preach about Jesus. "This man loves us," one of the people said. "And he himself practices what he teaches us to do." Unfortunately, the chief of this tribe was not happy with Father Peter's preaching. When the chief found out that his own son wanted to be baptized, he was furious. He sent a band of his warriors to kill the missionary. All the priest said as he lay dying was, "It is well with me." Father Peter Chanel was killed on April 28, 1841. Within a short time after his martyrdom, the whole island became Christian. Peter was declared a saint by Pope Pius XII in 1954.

We are all called to spread the Gospel of Jesus, each in our own way. The example of St. Peter shows us that practicing kindness and patience is the best way to bring the love of Jesus to others.

We also celebrate the feast of St. Louis Mary de Montfort on this day.

April 29

St. Catherine of Siena

Born in 1347, this well-known saint is the patroness of Italy, her country. Catherine was the youngest in a family of twenty-five children. Her mother and father wanted her to be happily married. But Catherine wanted very much to become a nun. To prove her point, she cut off her long, beautiful hair. She wanted to make herself unattractive. Her parents were very upset about this and scolded her frequently. They also gave her the heaviest housework to do. But Catherine did not back down. Finally, her parents stopped opposing her.

Catherine became closer and closer to Jesus. One night, when many people of Siena were out in the streets celebrating, Jesus appeared to Catherine who was praying alone in her room. With Jesus was his Blessed Mother. She took Catherine's hand and lifted it up to her Son. Jesus put a ring on Catherine's finger and she became his bride.

In Catherine's time, the Church had many problems. There were fights going on all over Italy. Catherine wrote letters to kings and queens. She even went to beg rulers to make peace with the pope and to avoid wars. Catherine asked the pope to leave Avignon, France, and return to Rome to guide the

Church. She told him it was God's will. He listened to Catherine and did what she said.

Catherine never forgot that Jesus was in her heart. Through her, Jesus helped the sick people she nursed. Through her Jesus comforted the prisoners she visited in jail.

This great saint died in Rome in 1380. She was just thirty-three years old. She was proclaimed a saint by Pope Pius II in 1461. In 1970, Pope Paul VI declared St. Catherine a Doctor of the Church. She received this great honor because she served Jesus' Church heroically during her brief lifetime.

Let's offer our whole hearts to God. Then, like St. Catherine, we'll discover how wonderful it is to love him! This love of God will also show in the way we treat other people.

April 30

St. Pius V

This holy pope was born in Italy in 1504. He was baptized Anthony Ghislieri. Anthony wanted to become a priest, but it seemed as though his dream would never come true. His parents were poor and didn't have enough money to send him to school. One day, two Dominicans came to his home and met Anthony. They were so impressed with him that they offered to educate him. And so at the age of fourteen, Anthony joined the Dominican Order. That is when he took the new name "Michael." Eventually, Michael became a priest. Then he became a bishop and cardinal.

Cardinal Michael courageously defended the teachings of the Church against those who opposed them. He continued to live a life of penance. When he was sixty-one, he was chosen pope. Again he took a new name— Pius V. He had once been a poor shepherd boy. Now he was the head of the whole Catholic Church. But he remained as humble as ever. He still wore his white Dominican habit, the same old one he had always worn. And no one could persuade him to change it.

Pope Pius V simplified the way things were done at the Vatican. He finished the new catechism of the Council of Trent and revised the prayer book used by priests and nuns every day and the missal used at Mass. He gave large sums of money to the poor, and personally visited hospitals and consoled the sick. Pope Pius V drew strength from the crucifix. He meditated every day on the sufferings and death of Jesus. He encouraged people to pray the rosary and established the feast of Our Lady of the Rosary. We celebrate it each year on October 7.

Pope Pius V died in Rome on May 1, 1572. Pius V was proclaimed a saint by Pope Clement XI in 1712.

The story of St. Pius V reminds us that the Lord chooses the people he wants for the jobs that he wants done. We are all very important to him because he is our Father. Let's keep in contact with God through our daily prayers and by receiving the sacraments of Holy Eucharist and Reconciliation often.

MAY

May 1

St. Joseph the Worker

This is St. Joseph's second feast day on the Church calendar of celebrations. We honor him also on March 19. St. Joseph is a very important saint. He is the husband of Mary and the foster-father of Jesus. Today we celebrate the witness of Joseph's hard work. He was a carpenter who labored long hours in his little shop. St. Joseph teaches us that the work we do is important. Through it we give our contribution and our service to our family and society. But even more than that, we follow God's plan for us by carrying out the special work he has given us to do. That is why we want to try to always do our work carefully and well.

Many countries set aside one day a year to honor workers. This encourages people to appreciate the dignity and importance of work. The Church has given us St. Joseph as a wonderful example to follow in doing our own work. In 1955, Pope Pius XII proclaimed that this feast of St. Joseph the Worker should be celebrated every year.

St. Joseph will be glad to help us become more conscientious in our study and our work if we ask him to. Let's always try our best, no matter what we're doing.

May 2

St. Athanasius

Athanasius was born around 297 in Alexandria, Egypt. He devoted his life to proving that Jesus is truly God. This was important because some people called Arians were denying this truth. Even before he became a priest, Athanasius had read many books on Scripture and theology. That is why he could explain the faith so easily.

This saint became the archbishop of Alexandria before he was thirty years old. For forty-six years, he was a brave shepherd of his flock. Four Roman emperors could not make him stop writing his clear and beautiful explanations of our holy faith. His enemies persecuted him in every way.

Archbishop Athanasius was sent out of his own diocese five times. His first exile lasted two years. He was sent to the city of Trier in Germany in 336. A kindly bishop, St. Maximinius, welcomed him warmly. Other exiles lasted longer. Athanasius was even hunted by people who wanted to kill him. During one tense exile, monks kept him hidden from his enemies in the desert for six years.

Once the emperor's soldiers were chasing Athanasius down the Nile River. "They're catching up to us!" cried the saint's friends. Athanasius was not worried. "Turn the boat around," he said calmly, "and row toward them."

The emperor's soldiers shouted, "Have you seen Athanasius?"

"You're not far from him!" Athanasius's friends shouted back. The enemy boat sped by them faster than ever, and the saint was safe.

The people of Alexandria loved their archbishop. He was a real father to them. As the years passed, they appreciated more and more how much he suffered for Jesus and the Church. It was the people who stepped in and saw to it that Athanasius had some well-deserved peace. He spent the last seven years of his life safe with them. His enemies searched for him but could never find him. During that time, Athanasius wrote *The Life of St. Anthony the Hermit.* Anthony had been his personal friend when Athanasius was young. (St. Anthony's feast day is celebrated on January 17.)

St. Athanasius died quietly on May 2, 373. He remains one of the greatest, bravest saints of all time.

Today's saint challenges us to be more enthusiastic about studying our faith. We can ask St. Athanasius to give us his love for Jesus. This love will lead us to want to know as much as we can about the Lord.

May 3

St. Philip and St. James

Both of these saints were part of the original group of Jesus' twelve apostles. Philip was one of the first apostles chosen. He was born at Bethsaida, in Galilee. When Jesus met him, he said, "Follow me." Philip was so happy to be with Jesus that he wanted to share his happiness with his friend, Nathaniel. "We have found the one Moses and the prophets wrote about," Philip explained. "He is Jesus of Nazareth."

Nathaniel wasn't at all excited. Nazareth was just a little village. It wasn't big and important like Jerusalem. So Nathaniel said, "Can any good come out of Nazareth?" But Philip did not become angry at his friend's answer. He just said, "Come and see." So Nathaniel went to see Jesus. After he had spoken with him, he, too, became a zealous follower of the Lord.

St. James was also one of Jesus' twelve apostles. He was the son of Alphaeus and a cousin of Jesus. After Jesus ascended into heaven, James became the bishop of Jerusalem. People thought so much of him that they called him "James the Just," which means "James the Holy One." He is also called "James the Less," because he was younger than the other apostle named James, who was called "James the Greater."

St. James was very gentle and forgiving. He prayed very much. He kept begging God to forgive the people who persecuted the followers of Jesus. Even when Jesus' enemies were putting James to death, he asked God to pardon them. St. James died as a martyr in the year 62.

We can all be apostles of Jesus in our own way. We can show our faith in Jesus by the way we live. That's how we can imitate St. Philip and St. James.

May 4

Blessed Ceferino Giménez Malla

Ceferino Giménez Malla was a gypsy (a member of a nomadic people who move from place to place) who was born in Spain in August of 1861. After they were married, he and his wife Teresa moved to Barbastro. They had no children of their own, but they adopted Teresa's niece, Pepita.

Ceferino was a horse trader who became well known for his fairness and his ability to settle disagreements. People who knew him were impressed by his kindness and prayerfulness. Even though he could not read or write, he was very wise, and even the bishop would come to him for advice. He was involved in his community as a city council member, and he also belonged to the Franciscan Third Order.

Ceferino lived at the time of the Spanish Civil War. Certain revolutionaries targeted anyone they suspected of siding with their opponents. This included the Catholic Church. A revolutionary movement called the Red Terror burned down churches and convents and put thousands of priests and nuns to death. One day, Ceferino noticed a young priest who was being bullied by some revolutionaries. In trying to defend the priest, Ceferino was arrested. Imprisoned for fifteen days, he remained strong in his faith and continued to pray, reciting the rosary each day. On August 9, 1936, he was taken to the cemetery of Barbastro and shot to death by a firing squad because he would not renounce his Catholic faith. Eighteen other people, mostly priests and religious, were put to death with him too. Ceferino was seventy-five years old.

Ceferino Giménez Malla was beatified on May 4, 1997, as the second lay martyr of the Spanish Civil War. He is the first gypsy to be beatified.

The story of Blessed Ceferino shows that all people are called by Jesus to lead holy lives. Our Church is made up of a wonderful variety of races and cultures. We should respect and appreciate them all.

St. Mary Mazzarello

Mary Mazzarello was born in 1837 near Genoa, Italy. She was the daughter of hardworking peasants, and she herself worked in the fields as a child. When she was seventeen, she joined a group of women devoted to our Lady. The group was called the Daughters of Mary Immaculate.

In 1860, Mary came down with a sickness called typhoid. She was no longer able to work in the fields. She decided to start a dressmaking business with her friend, Petronilla. The two young women would pray together as they did their sewing. They talked about a holy priest they knew named Don Bosco, who was working with boys who needed help. Soon they had the idea to begin a school for girls.

Don Bosco liked their idea and asked Pope Pius IX for permission to start a new order of sisters who would teach young girls. In 1872, Don Bosco (now known as St. John Bosco) founded the Daughters of Our Lady Help of Christians, also called the Salesian Sisters. Mother Mary Mazzarello became their superior. The community grew quickly. By 1900 there were nearly 800 convents and schools. The sisters carried out other works of charity in addition to their teaching ministry.

Blessed François de Montmorency Laval

Mother Mary Mazzarello died at the motherhouse at Nizza Monferrato on April 27, 1881. She was canonized by Pope Pius XII in 1951.

From her childhood, St. Mary Mazzarello did whatever work she had to do with great love. When she was unable to do one kind of work, she found something else she could do. Because she was ready to serve, God entrusted her with an important work in the Church.

May 6

St. Francois de Montmorency Laval

Francois was born in 1623 in a small town in France. He received a good Catholic education. He studied with the Jesuits and then went to Paris to complete his preparation for the priesthood. Francois became a priest in May, 1647, and a bishop on December 8, 1658. He arrived in Canada in 1659 to serve as Quebec's first bishop.

Bishop Laval had a missionary spirit. He shared the pioneer life of his people. He took on the huge task of organizing the Church in Canada, which was still mission territory. Bishop Laval asked the Jesuit missionaries to minister to the native people. He created new parishes for the French-speaking Catholics.

He started the Seminary of Quebec in 1663. This was of great importance because a good seminary would train future priests for God's people.

Bishop Laval loved the people of his vast territory. He was a caring bishop and a prayerful man. He spoke out against the harmful abuse of alcohol, which was a great problem in his area at that time. The way that the civil authorities constantly interfered with the life of the Church also made him suffer very much.

In 1688, Bishop Laval retired. He was replaced by Bishop de Saint-Vallier. Bishop Laval devoted the last twenty years of his life to charitable and spiritual works. He died in 1708. People came from all over to pray at his tomb, and miracles were reported. Pope Francis canonized Bishop Laval on April 3, 2014.

St. Francois helps us understand what it means to be a missionary. He had the courage to leave his own country to go to Canada when it was still a mission land. We can ask Blessed Francois to make us aware of the Church all around the world. Let's remember to pray that people in every country will come to learn about Jesus.

St. Rose Venerini

Rose was born in Viterbo, Italy, in 1656. Her father was a doctor. Rose entered the convent but returned home after a few months. Her father had died and she felt responsible for the care of her mother.

Rose, who would remain single, recognized her own leadership qualities. She gathered the young women in her neighborhood to pray the rosary in the evenings. As they all got to know each other, Rose became aware of how little the young people knew about their Catholic faith. Rose and two of her friends opened a free school for girls in 1685. The parents who sent their daughters there were very pleased with the quality of education and the atmosphere.

Rose was a gifted educator. Above all, she was able to teach others to teach. In 1692, Cardinal Barbarigo invited Rose to his diocese. He wanted her to organize his schools and train his teachers. It was in his diocese that she became a friend and teacher of Lucy Filippini. Lucy later started her own religious order and was proclaimed a saint in 1930.

Rose organized schools in various places. Some people didn't like her work, and they said unkind things about her and her teachers. But Rose never gave up. She even opened a school in Rome in 1713.

Pope Clement XI praised Rose for starting such a wonderful school.

This dedicated teacher died in Rome on May 7, 1728, at the age of seventy-two. After Rose's death, her group of teachers became a religious community known as the Venerini Sisters. They continue to teach in the spirit of Rose Venerini. Rose was declared "blessed" by Pope Pius XII in 1952. On October 15, 2006, Pope Benedict XVI canonized her.

St. Rose realized the value of education and dedicated her life to the teaching ministry. Today, think of a teacher who has made a difference in your life and thank God for her or him.

May 8

Blessed Catherine of St. Augustine

Catherine was born on May 3, 1632, in a little village in France. She was baptized the same day. Catherine came from a religious family. Her grandparents set a wonderful example for her, especially because of their genuine care for the poor. Catherine watched wide-eyed as her grandmother invited a handicapped beggar into her home. She offered him a bath, clean clothes, and a delicious meal. As Catherine and her grandparents sat around the fire that night, they prayed the *Our Father* out loud. They thanked God for his blessings.

Because there was no hospital in their small town, the sick were nursed back to health in the home of Catherine's grandparents. Catherine was just a little girl but she prayed to ask Jesus to make people suffer less.

When she was still quite young, Catherine joined a new order called the Sisters of St. Augustine. They took care of the sick in hospitals. Catherine received the religious habit on October 24, 1646. Her older sister pronounced her vows the same day. In 1648, Catherine listened to the missionary priests begging sisters to come to Canada, which was mission territory at that time. Catherine's sister was chosen to be one of the first sisters of their order to go as a missionary to Canada. Sister Catherine begged to be chosen too. She pronounced her vows on May 4, 1648. She sailed for Canada the very next day. It was the day before her sixteenth birthday.

Life was hard in Quebec, Canada. But Sister Catherine loved the people. The native people were so grateful for her cheerful ways. She cooked and cared for the sick in the order's simple hospital building. But Sister Catherine learned about fear, too. The Iroquois were killing people and burning villages. She prayed to St. John Brebeuf, one of the Jesuit priests who had recently been killed by the Iroquois in 1649. She asked him to help her be true to her calling. She heard him speaking in her heart, telling her to remain in Canada. Food became scarce, and the winters were terribly cold. Some of the sisters could not take the harsh life and constant fear of death. Sadly, they returned to France. Sister Catherine was afraid, too. She found it hard to pray. And while she smiled at all her patients at the hospital, she felt sad inside. It was then, when things were darkest for her, that Sister Catherine made a vow to remain in Canada, performing works of charity for the rest of her life. She was just twenty-two years old.

Despite the hard pioneer life of the French colony, more people came. The Church grew. God blessed the new land with more missionaries. In 1665, Sister Catherine became the novice directress of her community. She kept up her life of prayer and hospital ministry until her death. Sister Marie Catherine of St. Augustine died on May 8, 1668. She was thirty-six years old. She was declared "blessed" by Pope John Paul II in 1989.

Jesus never promised that our lives would be easy and without pain or trouble. But he did promise to be with us always. When we become afraid or downhearted, we can ask Blessed Catherine to help us to be as courageous as she was.

May 9

Blessed Nicholas Albergati

Nicholas was born in 1632 in Bologna, Italy. His family could afford to send him to the university where he began to study law. But after a few years, he decided not to become a lawyer. At the age of twenty, Nicholas joined the Carthusian Order. In 1417, he was chosen to be bishop of his native diocese. He had not counted on that at all. He could not even believe it could be God's will. But his superiors assured him it was.

People liked Bishop Nicholas. He lived in a small, plain house. He was like them. He began to visit the people of his diocese. He went to the poorest families first. He talked with them and helped them with their needs. He blessed their homes. The people were very grateful.

Bishop Nicholas became a cardinal in 1426. He was known to be wise and holy. Two popes, Martin V and Eugene IV, consulted him about important Church matters. Nicholas also encouraged learning. In fact, he wrote several books himself.

Bishop Nicholas died on May 9, 1443, while on a visit to Siena, Italy. Pope Eugene IV had his body brought back to Bologna. The pope himself participated in the funeral Mass and burial.

Do you ever feel upset when you don't get attention? That's the time to pray to Blessed Nicholas. He didn't even want the attention he received. Blessed Nicholas will show us how much better it is to spend our time praising God.

St. Damien Joseph de Veuster of Molokai

Joseph de Veuster was born in 1840, the son of Belgian farmers. He and his brother, Pamphile, joined the Fathers of the Sacred Hearts of Jesus and Mary. These missionaries were responsible for bringing the Catholic faith to the Hawaiian Islands.

Joseph chose the name "Damien" when he entered the Sacred Hearts Congregation. Brother Damien was tall and strong. His years of helping on the family farm had given him a healthy look. Everybody liked him because he was good-natured and generous.

More missionaries were needed in the kingdom of Hawaii (Hawaii was not a state at that time). In 1864, a group of Sacred Hearts priests and brothers were chosen to go. Pamphile, Damien's brother, was selected. Just before the departure date, Pamphile came down with typhoid fever. He could no longer consider going to the missions. Brother Damien, still studying to become a priest, asked to take his place. The father general accepted Damien's offer. Damien went home to his family to say goodbye. Then he took the ship from Belgium to Hawaii. The voyage lasted eighteen weeks. Damien finished his studies and was ordained a priest in Hawaii. He spent nine years among the people of three districts. He traveled on horseback and by canoe.

The people loved this tall, generous priest. He saw that they responded to ceremonies. He used the little money he could raise to build chapels. He and volunteer parishioners built the chapels themselves. But the most incredible part of Damien's life was soon to begin. The bishop asked for a volunteer priest to go to the island of Molokai. The very name struck the people with fear and dread. They knew that the section of the island called Kalawao was the "living graveyard" of people dying of leprosy. There was so much ignorance about the disease and such great fear of contagion that lepers were mostly abandoned. Many just despaired. There was no priest, no law enforcement agent on Molokai, no doctor or hospital. The Hawaiian government sent some food and medical supplies to the lepers, but it was not enough. And there was no organized way of distributing these goods.

Father Damien volunteered to go to Molokai. Faced with the poverty, corruption and despair, he felt afraid at first. But he made up his mind that for him there was no turning back. The people were desperately in need of help. He went to Honolulu to confront the members of the board of health. They told him that he could not travel back and forth to Molokai for fear of contagion. Their real reason was that they didn't want him on Molokai. They didn't want to be reminded that they were responsible for the lepers. So

Damien had to make a choice: if he went back to Molokai, he could never leave again. The board of health didn't know Damien. He chose Molokai.

Father Damien worked hard for eighteen years until his death on Molokai. With the help of the lepers and generous volunteers, Molokai was transformed. The word *Molokai* took on a whole different meaning. It became an island of Christian love. Father Damien eventually became a leper himself. He died on April 15, 1889, at the age of forty-nine and was buried on the island. He was proclaimed "blessed" by Pope John Paul II in 1994 and canonized by Pope Benedict XVI in 2009.

Let's ask St. Damien to give us some of his bravery and generosity. There are so many people who need our love and support. St. Damien will help us respond to them with joy and kindness.

May 11

St. Ignatius of Laconi

Ignatius was the son of a poor farmer in Laconi, Italy. He was born on December 17, 1701. When he was about seventeen, he became very ill. He promised to become a Franciscan if he would get better. But when the illness left him, his father convinced him to wait. A couple of years later, Ignatius was almost killed when he lost control of his horse. Suddenly, however, the horse stopped and trotted on quietly. Ignatius was convinced that God had saved his life. He made up his mind to follow his religious vocation at once, and he joined the Franciscans.

Brother Ignatius never held any important position in the Franciscan Order. For fifteen years he worked as a weaver. Then for forty years he carried out the task of asking for donations. He went from house to house requesting food and offerings to support the friars. Ignatius visited families and received their gifts. But the people soon realized that they received a gift in return. Brother Ignatius consoled the sick and cheered up the lonely. He made peace between enemies, converted people hardened by sin, and advised those in trouble. The people began to wait for his visits.

There were some difficult days too. Once in a while, a door was slammed in his face, and often the weather was bad. Always, there were miles and miles to walk. But Ignatius remained kind and faithful. He died at the age of eighty, on May 11, 1781. Ignatius was proclaimed a saint by Pope Pius XII in 1951.

St. Ignatius was a happy, dedicated Franciscan. He makes us realize that the best gift we can give anyone is our good example.

May 12

St. Pancras

Pancras, a fourteen-year-old orphan, lived in the late third century. He was not a native of Rome. He was brought there by his uncle who looked after him. Pancras became a follower of Jesus and was baptized. Although just a boy, he was arrested for being a Christian during the reign of the emperor Diocletian. Pancras refused to give up his faith. For that, he was sentenced to death and was beheaded. He became a very popular martyr in the early Church. People admired him for being so young and so brave. In 514, a large church was built in Rome to honor him. In 596, the famous missionary, St. Augustine of Canterbury, went to bring the Christian faith to England. He named his first church there after St. Pancras.

St. Pancras and the other martyrs we remember today remind us of the importance of our Catholic faith. It should mean as much to us as it did to each of them. If we need to grow stronger in our faith, let's ask St. Pancras to help us.

Today is also the feast day of St. Nereus and St. Achilleus.

May 13

Our Lady of Fatima

On May 13, 1917, three children were watching their sheep in a valley called the Cova da Iria, near the town of Fatima, in Portugal. They were ten-year-old Lucia dos Santos, and her cousins, nine-year-old Francisco and seven-year-old Jacinta Marto.

A flash of lightning suddenly startled them. The children thought a storm was coming, so they quickly began herding their sheep toward home. A second flash made them look around. They saw a beautiful young woman standing above a small oak tree. "Don't be afraid," she called reassuringly. "Come closer." The woman wore a robe and mantle of white, with gold trim. Her hands, joined in prayer, were holding a rosary. She shone with a light that was brighter than the sun.

Lucia asked the woman, "Who are you? What do you want?"

She answered, "I am from heaven. Come here on the thirteenth of each month for five months. On October 13, I will give a sign that will make everyone believe."

The Blessed Mother kept her promise. The children saw her once more on June 13 and July 13.

The mayor of the nearby town of Ourem didn't like this story of a heavenly lady appearing to children. On the morning of August 13, he offered Lucia and her cousins a ride to the Cova, where they were supposed to meet the lady again. But once he had them in his car, he brought them to the police station instead, and kept them in custody for two days. He couldn't outsmart the Blessed Virgin, though. She simply appeared to the children several days later!

A priest of the diocese questioned Lucia about the visions. How many times had they seen the Blessed Virgin? How long did she stay with them? What did she look like? Lucia answered all the questions. The priest also knew that Mary had told the children a secret. But he did not pressure Lucia to tell him what it was. Lucia told the priest a little prayer that Mary had taught them: "My Jesus, forgive us our sins. Save us from the fires of hell. Lead all souls to heaven, especially those in most need of your mercy."

The Blessed Virgin again visited the children at the Cova on September 13. On October 13, 1917, 70,000 people came to the Cova to witness the miracle that Mary had promised. It was a rainy day. But Lucia asked the people to close their umbrellas. The rain stopped. Mary appeared to the children. Suddenly, the clouds left the sky and the sun came out. The crowds saw it spinning and shooting out flames like a fireworks display. One by one the sun took on all the colors of the rainbow. This happened three times and the scene lasted for ten minutes. Then the sun seemed to fall from the sky toward the earth. The people fell to their knees. Many thought it was the end of the world. They wept and asked forgiveness for their sins. Suddenly the sun stopped its fall and returned to its normal color and its usual place in the sky.

While the sun had been spinning and changing colors, only Lucia, Francisco and Jacinta had seen Mary appear as Our Lady of the Rosary, with St. Joseph beside her holding the Child Jesus. Then Jesus alone appeared and blessed the crowd. Mary also appeared as Our Lady of Sorrows and then dressed as Our Lady of Mount Carmel. Mary told the children what she wanted: She asked that people pray the rosary and change their lives. They should ask forgiveness for sins. She also asked that a chapel be built at the Cova da Iria. The chapel was begun in 1919. Together with Lourdes, Fatima has become the most popular place of pilgrimage for Christians.

In December, 1918, both Francisco and Jacinta became very sick with the flu. In those days they didn't have the medicines we have today, and Francisco's illness turned into pneumonia. He died on April 4, 1919. A few months later, Jacinta's sickness developed into pleurisy, a disease which seriously affected her lungs. She underwent surgery, but died on February 20, 1920. Lucia entered the convent in 1928, becoming a Sister of St. Dorothy. In 1948 she transferred to the Carmelite monastery in Coimbra, Portugal. As of the date this book was printed, she is still living there as a Carmelite nun.

Our Lady came to Fatima as a loving mother. She wants us to be truly happy and reminds us that this can only happen when we live as Jesus taught. Let's pray the rosary often, thinking about the lives of Jesus and Mary.

May 14

St. Matthias

Matthias was one of the Lord's seventy-two disciples. He had been a follower of Jesus before the crucifixion. While waiting for the coming of the Holy Spirit, 120 of Jesus' followers gathered to pray. St. Peter asked them to choose an apostle to replace Judas. This was very important because that man would be a bishop, as the other apostles were. Peter said that they should choose someone who had been with Jesus from his baptism in the Jordan River until his resurrection.

The first chapter of the Acts of the Apostles tells us what happened. The group proposed two names. One was Matthias, the other was Joseph, also called Barsabbas. Then everyone prayed and asked the Lord to let them know which of the two men should take the place of Judas. Next they cast lots, and Matthias' name was chosen. He became one of the twelve apostles.

St. Matthias was a dedicated apostle. He preached the Good News in Judea, Cappadocia (modern-day Turkey), and on the Caspian seashore. Many people listened to Matthias. They believed his wonderful message. The enemies of Jesus grew furious when they saw how people listened to Matthias. They decided to stop him by putting him to death. Matthias died a martyr at Colchis.

The story of St. Matthias reminds us that we are fortunate to be followers of Jesus and members of his Church. Let's ask St. Matthias to show us how to be more grateful for all that we have received.

May 15

St. Isidore the Farmer

This saint was born in 1070, in Madrid, Spain. His parents were very religious. They named their baby after the great St. Isidore, archbishop of Seville, Spain. (We celebrated his feast on April 4.) Isidore's parents wanted to offer their son a good education, but they could not afford it because they were tenant farmers.

When Isidore was old enough, he went to work for a rich landowner in Madrid. This man's name was John de Vargas. Isidore worked all his life for Mr. de Vargas. He married a good woman named Maria Torribia, who was from a family as poor as his own. The couple loved each other very much. They had one child, a boy, who died as a baby. Isidore and his wife offered to Jesus their sadness over the child's death. They trusted that their son was happy with God forever.

Isidore began each day at Mass. Then he would go to his job. He tried to work hard even if he didn't feel like it. He plowed and planted and prayed. He called on Mary, the saints and his guardian angel. They helped him turn ordinary days into special, joyful times. The world of faith became very real to Isidore, as real as Mr. de Varga's fields. When he had a day off, Isidore made it a point to spend extra time adoring Jesus in church. Sometimes, on holidays, Isidore and Maria would visit a few neighboring parishes on a one-day pilgrimage of prayer.

Once the parish held a dinner. Isidore got there early and went into the church to pray. He arrived in the parish hall late. He didn't come in alone. He brought a group of beggars with him. The parishioners were upset. What if there wasn't enough food for all those beggars? But the more they filled up their plates, the more there was for everyone else! "There is always enough for the poor of Jesus," Isidore kindly explained.

Stories of miracles began to circulate about this farm-worker saint. Isidore was totally unselfish. He was a loving and compassionate human being. He is one of Spain's most popular saints. Isidore died on May 15, 1130. In March, 1622, Pope Gregory XV proclaimed five new saints in the same ceremony. They were St. Ignatius Loyola, St. Francis Xavier, St. Teresa of Avila, St. Philip Neri and St. Isidore the Farmer.

St. Isidore let his faith in Jesus and the Church light up his whole life. We can ask him to help us love the Lord and put our faith into practice as he did.

May 16

St. Felix of Cantalice

Felix was born in Cantalice, Italy, in 1515. His parents were poor peasants, and as a boy, Felix worked as a shepherd and then as a farm laborer. Even so, he managed to begin each day by attending Mass. As he worked in the fields, he prayed continually.

Felix joined the Capuchins in Anticoli. He soon became a model of prayer and penance, humility and charity. He was sent to the Capuchin monastery in Rome, where he spent the rest of his life helping to support his community by leaving his monastery every day and traveling through nearby towns asking for the necessary donations. The superiors were careful to choose a very holy brother who would not give in to greediness or be tempted to forget his daily prayers because he spent so much time outside the monastery. They trusted Brother Felix so much that he had permission to use some of the donations he collected to help the poor and sick people he met each day. One day a brother asked Brother Felix how he was not distracted by all the things he saw each day. Brother Felix answered, "Each creature in the world will lift our hearts to God if we look at it with a good eye."

While he was in Rome, Brother Felix became friends with St. Philip Neri. When St. Charles Borromeo asked St. Philip Neri's advice in revising the rule of life for his Oblates, St. Philip gave the book to Brother Felix and asked him to look it over. St. Charles was amazed at Brother Felix's insights and grateful for his help.

Brother Felix died on May 18, 1587, when he was seventy-two years old. He was canonized in 1709.

St. Felix teaches us that we can be united to God in any place and at any time. Whether we find ourselves in a quiet church or on a busy street, we can always raise our minds and hearts to God.

May 17

St. Paschal Baylon

Paschal, a Spanish saint, was born in 1540. From the time he was seven, he worked as a shepherd. He never had the opportunity to go to school. Yet he taught himself to read and write. He did this mainly by asking everyone he met to help him. He wanted to learn to read religious books. As he tended sheep each day, he would also spend his time praying.

When he was twenty-four, Paschal became a Franciscan brother. Paschal was kind and easy to get along with. His companions liked him. They noticed that he often chose the hardest and most unpleasant chores. He was known for his spirit of penance. Yet he was a happy person. As a shepherd, Paschal had wished he could be in church, praying to Jesus. At that time he couldn't. Now he could. He loved to keep Jesus in the Blessed Sacrament company. He considered it an honor to be a server at Mass.

Brother Paschal's two great loves were the Holy Eucharist and the Blessed Mother. Every day Paschal prayed the rosary with great love. He also wrote beautiful prayers to our heavenly Mother.

Paschal made himself a little notebook out of some scraps of paper. In it, he wrote down some beautiful thoughts and prayers. After he died, his superior showed the little book to the archbishop. The archbishop read the book and said, "These simple souls are stealing heaven from us!"

Paschal died in 1592 at the age of fifty-two. He was proclaimed a saint by Pope Alexander VIII in 1690.

What does it take to be a saint? St. Paschal had the strength to live his religious vocation because of his devotion to Jesus in the Holy Eucharist and the Blessed Mother. Let's ask St. Paschal to help us grow closer to Jesus and Mary.

St. John I

John I was a priest of Rome. He became pope after the death of Pope St. Hormisdas in 523. At that time, Italy's ruler was Theodoric the Goth, an Arian. (The Arians did not believe that Jesus is God.)

In 523 Emperor Justin of Constantinople decreed that the Arians had to give back to the Catholics the church buildings they had taken. This made Theodoric angry. He forced Pope John to go with a delegation of five bishops and four senators to speak to the emperor. The emperor and all the people of Constantinople went out to meet the pope with a joyful welcome. Justin listened to Pope John, and decided to change his harsh policy.

But Theodoric was not satisfied. He imagined there was a conspiracy against him. He thought that Pope John and Justin I were against him. When the pope was returning to Rome he was kidnapped in Ravenna, Theodoric's capital. Pope John was thrown into prison by Theodoric's soldiers. There the pope died of thirst and starvation in 526.

When we're tempted to have mean thoughts about others, we can pray to St. John. He'll help us avoid Theodoric's terrible mistake of acting upon our angry or jealous thoughts.

May 19

St. Celestine V

Peter di Morone was the eleventh of twelve children. He was born around 1210 in Isernia, Italy. His father died when he was small. The family was poor, but Peter's mother raised her children with great love. She sent Peter to school because he showed such promise and an eagerness to learn. Once she asked, "Which one of you is going to become a saint?" Little Peter answered with all his heart, "Me, Mama! I'll become a saint!"

When he was twenty, Peter became a hermit. He spent his days praying, reading the Bible and doing his work. Other hermits kept coming to him and asking him to guide them. Eventually, he started a new order of monks.

When Peter was eighty-four years of age, he was made pope. It came about in a very unusual way. For two years there had been no pope. This was because the cardinals could not agree on whom to choose. Peter sent them a message. He warned them to decide quickly, because God was not pleased with the long delay. The cardinals did as the monk said. Then and there, they chose Peter the hermit to be the pope! The poor man wept when he heard the news. He accepted sadly and took the name Celestine V.

He was pope for only about four months. Because he was so humble and simple, King Charles of Naples and others took advantage of him. Trusting too much in others, Pope Celestine did whatever they suggested. Soon there was great confusion. Pope Celestine felt responsible for all the trouble. He decided that the best thing he could do for the Church was give up his position. He asked forgiveness for not having governed the Church well.

All St. Celestine wanted was to live in one of his monasteries in peace. But the new pope, Boniface VIII, thought it would be safer to keep him hidden in a small room in one of the Roman palaces. St. Celestine spent the last ten months of his life in a plain room. But he became his cheerful self again. "All I wanted in this world was a cell, and that is what they have given me," he would repeat to himself. He died on May 19, 1296. He was proclaimed a saint by Pope Clement V in 1313.

St. Celestine was a great monk. The way he handled his painful time as pope proved that he really was holy. He shows us that when we try our best, we can leave the results up to God and be in peace.

St. Bernardine of Siena

St. Bernardine of Siena was born in 1380 in a town near Siena, Italy. He was the son of an Italian governor. His parents died when he was seven, and his aunt took him in and raised him. She loved him as if he were her own child. His relatives also gave him a good education. He grew up to be a tall, handsome boy. He was so much fun that his friends loved to be with him. Yet they knew better than to use bad language when he was around. He would not allow it.

This saint had a special love for the Blessed Mother. She was the one who kept him pure. Even when he was a teenager, Bernardine would pray to her as a child talks to his mother.

Bernardine had a kind heart. He felt great pity for the poor. Once his aunt had no extra food to give a beggar. The boy cried, "I'd rather go without food myself than leave that poor man with none." When a plague struck the area in 1400, Bernardine and his friends volunteered their services at the hospital. They helped the sick and dying day and night for four months until the plague had ended.

Bernardine joined the Franciscan Order when he was twenty-two. He became a priest. After several years, he was assigned to go to towns and cities to preach. The people needed to be reminded about the love of Jesus. Bad habits were ruining both young and old people. "How can I save these people by myself?" Bernardine asked the Lord in prayer. "With what weapons can I fight the devil?" And God answered, "My Holy Name will be enough for you." So Bernardine spread devotion to the Holy Name of Jesus. He used this Name a great many times in every sermon. He asked people to print Jesus' name over the gates of their cities, over their doorways—everywhere. Through devotion to the Holy Name of Jesus and devotion to the Blessed Mother, Bernardine brought thousands of people from all over Italy back to the Church.

St. Bernardine spent forty-two years of his life as a Franciscan. He was offered the opportunity to become a bishop three times, but declined each time. In 1430 he was elected vicar general and for twelve years he worked to reform his Order. As a result of his efforts, the number of members grew from three hundred to over four thousand! He died at the age of sixty-four in Aquila, Italy, on May 20, 1444. He was declared a saint just six years later, in 1450, by Pope Nicholas V.

St. Bernardine devoted himself to serving Jesus and making everyone love his holy name. We can learn from him to respect the Lord's name and avoid the habit of using bad language.

St. Christopher Magallanes

The beginning of the twentieth century was a time of social problems and political unrest in Mexico. With the Constitution of 1917, the Mexican government sought to drive the Catholic Church out of the country. But many devout Catholics continued to practice their faith in secret. And many dedicated Mexican priests risked their lives in ministering to the underground or hidden Church.

Padre Christopher Magallanes was one of those priests. He belonged to the Cristeros Movement. This was an organization of Catholic priests and laypeople who had the courage to stand up to the anti-Catholic government during the 1920s. Padre Magallanes opened an underground seminary at Totatiche. Here with other priests he preached the Gospel in secret and celebrated Mass for the faithful. The people knew they could go to Padre Christopher to receive the sacraments and to be strengthened in their faith during those difficult times of persecution.

Government authorities finally arrested Padre Christopher Magallanes and put him in prison. People could hear their beloved priest cry out with conviction from his jail cell, "I am innocent and I will die innocent! With all my heart I forgive those responsible for my death, and I ask God that the shedding of my blood will bring peace to our divided Mexico!"

Padre Christopher was put to death with twenty-one other diocesan priests and three laymen. They were all members of the Cristeros Movement.

Pope John Paul II canonized Padre Christopher and the other martyrs on May 21, 2000.

St. Christopher will help us to be true to our faith, even when it doesn't seem "popular." His story also helps us to be grateful that we are able to practice our faith in freedom.

May 22

St. Rita of Cascia

Rita was born in 1381 in a little Italian village. Her parents, who were elderly, had begged God to send them a child. They loved Rita and brought her up well. When she was twelve, Rita wanted to enter the convent, but her parents decided that she should marry instead. The man they chose for Rita turned out to be a cruel and angry husband. He had such a violent temper that everyone in the neighborhood was afraid of him. Yet for eighteen years his wife patiently put up with his insults. Her prayers, gentleness and goodness finally won his heart. He apologized to Rita for the way he had treated her and he was very sorry. Rita's happiness over her husband's conversion did not last long. One day, shortly after, he was murdered. Rita was shocked and heartbroken. But she forgave the murderers, and tried to make her two sons forgive them too. She saw that the boys, instead, were determined to avenge their father's death. Rita prayed that they would not commit murder. Within several months, both boys became seriously ill. Rita nursed them lovingly. During their illness, she persuaded them to forgive, and to ask God's forgiveness for themselves. They did, and both died peacefully.

Now that her husband and her children were dead, Rita asked several times to enter the convent of the Augustinian nuns in Cascia. But the rules of the convent did not permit a woman who had been married to join even if her husband had died. Rita didn't give up, however. At last the nuns made an exception for her. In the convent, Rita stood out for her prayer, mortification and charity. She had great devotion to the crucified Jesus. Once, while praying in front of a crucifix, she asked Jesus to let her share some of his pain. One thorn from Jesus' crown of thorns pierced her forehead and made a wound that never healed. In fact, it grew so bad that Rita had to stay away from the other sisters, who were afraid of contagion. But she was happy to suffer to show her love for Jesus.

Rita died on May 22, 1457, when she was seventy-six. Like St. Jude, St. Rita is often called the "Saint of the Impossible."

Maybe someone we know and love is not living close to God. We can ask St. Rita to help us know how to pray for that person. Our kindness and understanding can be a reflection of God's love for that person.

May 23

St. John Baptist Rossi

John Baptist Rossi was born in 1698 in a village near Genoa, Italy. His family loved him. They were grateful when a wealthy couple that they knew hired John to serve in their household. John was happy to go to their house in Genoa because then he could attend school. When he was thirteen, he began studying for the priesthood at the Roman College. He realized that studies were easy for him and he signed up for more and more subjects.

Then John became very sick and had to stop his studies for a while. After he recovered enough, he completed his preparation and became a priest. Even though his health was always poor, Father John did much good for the people of Rome. He knew what it was like not to feel well, so he took a special interest in sick people. He was a frequent visitor to Rome's hospitals. Father John especially loved to spend time with the poor people at the Hospice of St. Galla. This was a shelter for the poor and homeless. But Father

John became aware of poor people who had no one to look after their spiritual needs. He noticed those who brought cattle and sheep to sell at the market. What hard lives they had. They came in the morning with their herds. Father John would walk among them and stop and talk with them. When possible, he would teach them about the faith and offer them the sacrament of Reconciliation. Father John's priestly ministry made a big difference in their lives.

The priest also felt a deep compassion for the homeless women and girls. They wandered through the streets day and night begging. This was dangerous and very sad. The pope gave Father John money to open a shelter for homeless women. It was right near the hospice of St. Galla. Father John placed the house under the protection of one of his favorite saints, Aloysius Gonzaga. (The feast of St. Aloysius is June 21.) Father John became best known for his kindness and gentleness in confession. People formed lines near his confessional and waited patiently for their turn. He once said to a friend that the best way for a priest to reach heaven was to help people through the sacrament of Reconciliation. Another favorite assignment given him by Pope Benedict XIV was to teach courses of spiritual instruction to prison officials and state employees.

Father John suffered a stroke in 1763. He never regained his health. He was able to celebrate Mass but he suffered greatly. This wonderful priest died at the age of sixty-six. It was May 23, 1764. He was proclaimed a saint by Pope Leo XIII in 1881.

We can learn from the life of St. John Baptist to be grateful for priests and for the sacrament of Reconciliation. We can also pray to this saint and ask him to console priests for all the good they do.

May 24

Blessed Marie-Leonie Paradis

Elodie Paradis was born on May 12, 1840, in the village of L'Acadie in Quebec, Canada. Her parents were poor and devout Catholics. They loved their little girl. When Elodie was nine, her parents decided to send her to a boarding school. They wanted her to have an excellent education. The sisters of Notre Dame warmly received the new student. But Elodie and her family missed each other very much.

Mr. Paradis worked hard running a mill. But times were bad, and there was not enough work to support his wife and children. He heard wonderful reports of the gold rush in California. He was so desperate that he decided to go. In California, Mr. Paradis did not find the wealth he had hoped for. When he returned to L'Acadie, he was shocked to find that his Elodie had entered the convent. She had joined the Holy Cross congregation on February 21, 1854. Mr. Paradis went to the convent. He begged his daughter to return home, but she chose to remain. Finally, her father accepted her decision. Elodie pronounced her vows in 1857, taking the name Sister Marie-Leonie. She taught school in different cities. She prayed and lived her life joyfully.

As time went on, Sister Marie-Leonie was led by Jesus to begin a new religious order in the Church. The Little Sisters of the Holy Family were begun in 1880. These loving sisters are devoted to the priesthood. They do the household tasks so that priests will be able to devote more time to their people. The Little Sisters of the Holy Family now have many convents in Canada, the United States, Rome and Honduras.

Mother Marie-Leonie worked for her sisters until the last few hours of her life. She was always frail and often ill. But she never stopped caring for God's people. She put the finishing touches on the pages of the rule of life she had written. She had it sent to the print shop. That book would give her sisters the guidance they would need to live their religious life. On Friday, May 3, 1912, Mother Marie-Leonie said she felt very tired. She went to rest and died a few hours later. She was seventy-one years old.

Mother Marie-Leonie was declared "blessed" by Pope John Paul II. The joyful event took place at Jarry Park, Montreal, Canada, on September 11, 1984.

Little tasks that seem unimportant can be worth a lot when they're done with love. When we are carrying out chores that seem boring or insignificant, let's offer them to God with the same spirit Blessed Marie-Leonie had in doing her work.

St. Bede the Venerable

This saint is famous as a priest, a monk, a teacher and a writer of history. He was born in England around 672. His parents sent Bede to school at the nearby Benedictine monastery. He loved the life of the monks so much that when he grew up he too became a monk. He remained in that same monastery for the rest of his life.

Bede loved the Holy Bible very much. He tells us that it was a joy for him to study the Bible. He loved to teach it and write about it. When he grew older, sickness forced him to stay in bed. His pupils came to study by his bedside. He kept on teaching them and working on his translation of St. John's Gospel into English. Many people could not read Latin. He wanted them to be able to read the words of Jesus in their own language.

As he grew sicker, Bede realized that he was about to go back to God. The monks would miss him very much. He kept on working even when he was seriously ill. At last, the boy who was doing the writing for him said, "There is still one sentence, dear Father, which is not written down." "Write it quickly," answered the saint. When the boy said, "It is finished," the saint said, "Good! You are right—it is finished. Now please hold my head up. I want to sit facing the place where I used to pray. I want to call on my heavenly Father."

Bede died shortly after, on May 25, 735. He is thought to be the most learned man of his time. His most famous book, *Church History of the English People,* is the only source for much of early English history. People call Bede by the respectful title of "venerable." He is also a Doctor of the Church.

If St. Bede were alive today, how much time do you think he would spend watching TV? How much time do you spend in front of the TV set each day? What adjustments can you make to allow time for important things like study, playing with friends, good reading and household chores?

Today is also the feast day of St. Gregory VII and St. Mary Magdalen de Pazzi.

May 26

St. Philip Neri

St. Philip Neri was born in Florence, Italy, in 1515. As a child, his nickname was "Good little Phil." He was always so cheerful and friendly that everyone he met loved him. Philip went to Rome as a teenager. He studied theology and philosophy for three years and was a good student. Above all, Philip was a very active Christian. He lived simply and worked hard. But he also did much good for the people around him. He helped poor children. He donated his time to the sick. He was a friend to people who were troubled and lonely. In fact, he reached out to everybody he could for the love of Jesus.

Philip helped start an organization of lay people to take care of needy pilgrims. That ministry gradually continued as a famous hospital in Rome. The priest who guided him realized that Philip was doing so much to help the Christians of Rome become fervent again. But it was obvious that Philip had the call to be a priest. He was ordained in 1551, at the age of thirty-six, and quickly became sought after as a confessor. He was available for the sacrament of Reconciliation for several hours every day. The lines of people who came to him grew longer. But Father Philip was never in a hurry. He never ran out of patience and gentleness.

People began to notice that he could read their minds at times. He could also in some circumstances predict the future. The Lord even worked miracles through him. But all Philip wanted to do was bring Jesus to the people. To avoid their admiration, he acted silly once in a while. He wanted people to laugh and forget that they thought he was holy.

Philip was making a difference in Rome. He founded a society of priests called the Oratorians, and the whole city was renewing its faith and devotion. Once he started to think about being a missionary to far-off lands. He was very impressed by the life of St. Francis Xavier, who had died in 1552 at the gate of China.

Philip had been a priest for just one year at the time of St. Xavier's death. Should he leave Rome and volunteer for the missions? A holy Cistercian monk told him, "Rome is to be your mission land." In fact, Father Philip had become known as "the apostle of Rome."

Philip spent the last five years of his life offering the sacrament of Reconciliation to the people. He died at the age of eighty in 1595. He was proclaimed a saint by Pope Gregory XV in 1622.

Cheerfulness is an important part of holiness. St. Philip Neri's story teaches us that the way to be really happy is to put God and other people first in our lives. If we only think about ourselves we'll never feel satisfied.

May 27

St. Augustine of Canterbury

Augustine was the abbot of St. Andrew's monastery in Rome. Pope Gregory the Great chose him and forty other monks for an important mission. They were to go and preach the Gospel to the people of England. Abbot Augustine and the monks started on their journey. When they reached southern France, people warned them that the English were fierce. The monks felt discouraged. They asked Augustine to go back and obtain the pope's permission to give up the whole idea. He did, but the pope wanted the monks to go to England just the same. Pope Gregory knew that the people were ready to accept the Christian faith. And so the monks continued their journey. They arrived in England in 597.

The monks were kindly received by King Ethelbert, whose wife was a Christian princess from France. The monks formed a procession when they arrived. They walked along singing psalms. They carried a cross and a picture of our Lord. Many people welcomed the monks' message. King Ethelbert himself was baptized on Pentecost, 597. That year Abbot Augustine became a bishop.

Augustine often wrote to the pope. And Pope St. Gregory gave him much holy advice. Speaking about the many miracles Augustine worked, the pope said: "You must rejoice with fear and fear with joy for that gift." He meant that Augustine should be happy that through the miracles the English people were putting faith in the Gospel. But he should be careful not to take credit for the miracles, because they were from God.

At Canterbury, Augustine built a church and a monastery, which became the most important in England. St. Augustine died on May 26, 604, seven years after his arrival in England.

If our parents or teachers ask us to do something that seems difficult or uninteresting, we should do it as best as we can. St. Augustine will help us because he knows how it feels to be given a difficult assignment.

May 28

St. Mariana of Quito

Mariana de Paredes y Flores was born at Quito, Ecuador, in 1618. At that time Ecuador was part of Peru. Mariana's parents were Spanish nobles, but they died when she was a child. Mariana's married sister took her into her home and raised her.

From her early years, Mariana was drawn to a life of prayer. She chose to stay at home, doing humble chores and devoting her time to prayer and acts of penance. She placed herself under the guidance of a Jesuit priest.

Mariana became known for her holiness of life. She had the gift of prophecy and worked miracles. In 1645, Quito was badly shaken by an earthquake. This was followed by an epidemic. Mariana offered her life to make up for the sins of the people of Quito. As soon as she made her offering, the epidemic came to an end. Mariana died on May 26 of the same year.

The people of Ecuador lovingly call St. Mariana the "Lily of Quito." She was canonized in 1950.

St. Mariana can help us to have faith in the power of prayer and penance. There are many needs to pray for in the world today. We can do our part by offering up prayers and little sacrifices for the needs of others.

May 29

St. Eugene de Mazenod

Eugene was born in France in 1782. He became a priest in 1811. Father Eugene was sensitive to the needs of the poor, and he ministered to them. He was always eager to find new ways to reach out to young people, too. He wanted to bring them to the love and practice of their faith. Father Eugene believed in the value of parish missions. He realized that missionary priests in a parish could help the people to better love and appreciate their Catholic faith.

Father Eugene began a new religious order of priests and lay brothers in 1816. They were missionaries called the Oblates of Mary Immaculate. Their special work was to go to people who had never heard of Jesus and his Church. Father Eugene and the members of his order were courageous in answering the requests of bishops who needed their help. Bishop Ignace Bourget of Montreal was especially eager to have their help. He must have been very convincing because Father Eugene sent several of his members to Montreal. Within ten years, the Oblates had grown rapidly. They reached all of Canada and had begun to minister in the United States, too.

In 1837, Father Eugene was consecrated bishop of Marseilles, France. He became known for his loyalty and love for the pope. He was also a gifted organizer and educator. Bishop Eugene remained superior of his order until he died in 1861.

The great work Bishop Eugene de Mazenod started continues today through the Oblate missionaries around the world. They staff many mission posts, parishes and universities.

St. Eugene had the courage to respond to the needs of God's people as he saw them. Let's ask him to show us how we too can help the people around us.

May 30

St. Joan of Arc

Joan was born in 1412. Her hometown was Domremy, a little village in France. Jacques d'Arc, her father, was a hardworking farmer. Her mother was gentle and loving. She taught Joan many practical things so that Joan could later say, "I can sew and spin as well as any woman." Joan loved to pray, especially at the shrines of our Blessed Mother. But this honest little peasant girl was to become a heroine....

One day while Joan was watching her sheep, St. Michael the Archangel, the patron of her country, told her, "Daughter of God, go save France!" For three years she heard the voices of saints calling her to action. When she was sixteen, she began her mission.

At that time, there was a war going on between France and England. It was called the Hundred Years' War. England had won so much French land that the king of England called himself the king of France, too. The real French king was weak and selfish. He thought that the French armies would never be able to save the country.

After being examined by many priests and experts to make sure that she really *was* seeing visions of the saints and really *had* been given a special mission to carry out, Joan received permission to lead an army into the French city of Orleans, which the English had almost captured. In her white, shining armor, this young teenager rode with her banner flying above her. On it were the names of JESUS and MARY. Joan was wounded by an arrow in the great battle of Orleans, but she kept on urging the men in her army to victory. At last they won! Then Joan and her army went on to win more and more battles. The English armies had to retreat.

After the victories, Joan's time of suffering began. She was captured and sold to the British. The ungrateful French king did not even try to save her. She was put in prison and falsely charged with witchcraft and heresy (denying or doubting a truth of the Catholic faith). After an unfair trial Joan was burned at the stake on May 29, 1431. Joan was not even twenty, yet she went bravely to her death. The last word on her lips was "Jesus." Four hundred and eighty-nine years later, on May 16, 1920, Pope Benedict XV proclaimed Joan a saint.

St. Joan was asked by God to accomplish a very difficult, nearly impossible task. She trusted God and did what he asked. When we have to do something hard, we can ask St. Joan to help us.

May 31

Visitation of the Blessed Virgin Mary

When the archangel Gabriel announced to the Blessed Virgin Mary that she was to be the mother of the Savior, he also told Mary that her cousin Elizabeth was going to have a baby. Elizabeth was an older woman. Mary knew that she would appreciate some help. So she started out at once on the journey to Elizabeth's house.

Mary's trip was long and dangerous. Riding on a donkey, it was uncomfortable too. But that didn't stop her. Mary reached her cousin's house and greeted Elizabeth. At that moment, God revealed to Elizabeth that Mary had become his mother. Elizabeth asked joyfully, "How have I deserved that the mother of my Lord should come to me?" Mary remained humble. She quickly gave all the credit to God. She exclaimed: "My soul magnifies the Lord, and my spirit rejoices in

God my Savior, for he has regarded the lowliness of his handmaid, and holy is his name."

What graces the Blessed Mother brought to the home of her cousin! St. John the Baptist, while still hidden in his mother's womb, was cleansed of original sin. Zachary, Elizabeth's husband, who had become mute for doubting the angel of God, was able to speak again. And Elizabeth was filled with the gifts of the Holy Spirit.

Mary stayed three months at her cousin's home. With great kindness and love, she helped Elizabeth. It was a wonderful time for them both.

Elizabeth's home was filled with grace through Mary's visit. We will receive many blessings too if we love and pray to our heavenly Mother.

JUNE

June 1

St. Justin

Justin was from Samaria. He lived in the second century. His father brought him up without any belief in God. When he was a boy, Justin studied poetry, history and science. As he grew up, he kept on studying because he wanted to find out the truth about God.

One day as he was walking along the shore of the sea, Justin met an old man. They began to talk together. Since Justin looked troubled, the man asked him what was on his mind. Justin answered that he was unhappy because he had not found anything certain about God in all the books he had read. The old man told him about Jesus, the Savior. He encouraged Justin to pray so that he would be able to understand the truth about God.

So Justin began to pray and to read the Word of God, the Bible. He grew to love it very much. He was also impressed to see how brave the Christians were who died for their belief in and love for Jesus. After learning more about the Christian religion, Justin became a Christian when he was about thirty years old. Then he used his great knowledge to explain and defend the faith with many writings.

Justin went to Rome and began teaching there. It was in Rome that he was arrested for being a Christian. The judge asked him, "Do you think that by dying you will enter heaven and be rewarded?" "I don't just think so," the saint answered. "I am sure of it!" And he died a martyr around the year 166.

To keep our faith strong like St. Justin's we can pray an act of faith often. A short one that's easy to remember is: "My God, I believe in you."

June 2

St. Marcellinus and St. Peter

These two saints are mentioned in the First Eucharistic Prayer of the Mass. They were widely honored and prayed to by the early Christians. The feast of these two martyrs was included in the Roman calendar of saints by Pope Vigilius in 555.

Marcellinus was a priest. Peter assisted him in his ministry. Both were very brave in the practice of their Christian faith. They served the Christian community with great self-sacrifice. During the persecution of Diocletian, many Christians were killed. Marcellinus and Peter were martyred in 304. As they awaited execution in prison, they continued to witness to their faith in Jesus. Many people, including their jailer and his family, were impressed by their strong faith and became Christians too. When the time came for their execution, Marcellinus and Peter were brought to a hidden spot in a forest called Silva Nigra. This was done to keep the Christians from finding them. Marcellinus and Peter were put to work clearing the briars away to prepare the place where they would be buried. Then they were beheaded. Some time later, their executioner was sorry for the terrible thing he had done. He led the Christians to the graves. Then Marcellinus and Peter were buried in the catacomb of St. Tiberius. Pope Gregory IV sent their relics to Frankfurt, Germany, in 827. He believed that the relics of these two saints would bring blessings to the Church in that nation.

We can learn from the martyrs that our lives should show that we believe in and love Jesus. Let's pray to St. Marcellinus and St. Peter and ask them for the grace to grow in our faith and love.

St. Charles Lwanga and Companions

Christianity was still quite new to Uganda, Africa, when a Catholic mission was started there in 1879. The priests were members of the Missionaries of Africa. Because of their white religious habit, they became popularly known as the "White Fathers."

King Mwanga did not understand Christianity. But he became angry when Joseph Mkasa, the teacher of the court pages and a Catholic, denounced him for his corrupt way of life. The king had murdered a Protestant minister. He had also been committing sins against purity with his young court pages. King Mwanga's anger turned into resentment and hatred for Joseph Mkasa and his Catholic religion. A few of the king's ambitious officers fueled his fears with lies. Joseph Mkasa was beheaded on November 18, 1885. The persecution had begun. Before it was over, a hundred people died. Twenty-two of them would be declared saints.

With the death of Joseph Mkasa, Charles Lwanga took his place as master of the king's pages. On May 26, 1886, the king found out that some of his pages were Catholic. He called in Denis Sebuggawo. He asked Denis if he had been teaching religion to another page. Denis said yes. The king grabbed his spear and flung it violently through the young man's throat. Then the king shouted that no one was permitted to leave his headquarters. War drums beat throughout the night. In a hidden room, Charles Lwanga secretly baptized four pages. One was St. Kizito, a cheerful, generous thirteen-year-old. He was the youngest of the group.

Most of the twenty-two Uganda martyrs who have been proclaimed saints were killed on June 3, 1886. They were forced to walk thirty-seven miles to the execution site. After a few days in prison, they were thrown into a huge fire. Seventeen of the martyrs were royal pages. One of the martyred boys was St. Mbanga. His own uncle was the executioner that day. Another of the martyrs, St. Andrew Kaggwa, died on January 27, 1887. He was among the twenty-two proclaimed saints in 1964 by Pope Paul VI.

St. Charles Lwanga is the patron of African young people. He and his companions really appreciated their gift of faith and refused to give it up. They were heroes! St. Charles and the Ugandan martyrs show us how to witness to Jesus and his Church.

June 4

St. Francis Caracciolo

Francis was born in the Abruzzi region of Italy on October 13, 1563. His father was a Neapolitan prince.

His mother was related to the Aquino family to which the thirteenth-century saint, Thomas Aquinas, belonged. Francis had a good upbringing. He was active in sports. But when he was twenty-two, a disease similar to leprosy, brought him close to death. While he was sick, he thought about the emptiness of the pleasures of the world. He realized that real happiness could only be found in something deeper. Francis made a vow that if he got better, he would dedicate his life to God. He recuperated so quickly that it seemed like a miracle. Francis kept his promise. He began his studies to become a priest.

After being ordained, Father Francis joined a group who were devoted to prison ministry. They cared for the prisoners and prepared condemned men to die reconciled to God. Francis and another priest, John Augustine Adorno, started a new religious congregation called the Minor Clerics Regular. When Father John died, Francis was chosen as the superior or leader of the group. He was not at all comfortable with this position. In fact, he was so humble that he actually signed his letters, "Francis the sinner." He also took his turn, along with the other priests, sweeping the floors, making beds and washing dishes.

Father Francis often spent almost the whole night praying in church. He wanted all the priests to spend at least one hour a day in prayer before the Blessed Sacrament. Francis spoke so often and so well about God's love for us that he became known as "the preacher of the love of God."

Francis did not live a long life. He died in June, 1608, at the age of forty-four. Just before he died, he suddenly cried, "Let's go!" "Where do you want to go?" asked the priest by his bed. "To heaven! To heaven!" came the answer in a clear, happy voice. Francis Caracciolo was proclaimed a saint by Pope Pius VII in 1807.

In his second letter to the Corinthians, St. Paul reminds us that "God loves the cheerful giver." This was the kind of person St. Francis was. We can ask him to help us to be generous in cheerfully offering our help to others.

June 5

St. Boniface

This great apostle of Germany was born in Devonshire, England, around the year 680. When he was small, some missionaries stayed a while at his home. They told the boy all about their work. They were so happy and excited about bringing the Good News to people. Boniface decided in his heart that he would be just like the missionaries when he grew up.

While still young, Boniface went to a monastery school to be educated. Some years later, he became a popular teacher. When he was ordained a priest, he was a powerful preacher because he was so full of enthusiasm.

Boniface wanted everyone to have the opportunity to know about and love Jesus and his Church. He became a missionary to the western part of Germany. Pope St. Gregory II blessed him and sent him on this mission. Boniface preached with great success. He was gentle and kind. He was also a man of great courage. Once, to prove that the pagan gods were false, he did a bold thing. There was a certain huge oak tree called the "oak of Thor." The pagans believed it was sacred to their gods. In front of a large crowd, Boniface cut down the tree with an axe. The big tree crashed. The pagans realized that their gods were false when nothing happened to Boniface.

Everywhere he preached, new members were received into the Church. In his lifetime, Boniface converted great numbers of people. In place of the statues of the pagan gods, he built churches and monasteries. In 732, the new pope, St. Gregory III, made Boniface an archbishop and gave him another mission territory. It was Bavaria, which is part of Germany today. Boniface and some companions went there to teach the people about the Christian faith. Here, too, the holy bishop was very successful.

Then, one day, Bishop Boniface was preparing to confirm some converts. A group of fierce warriors swooped down on the camp. Boniface would not let his companions defend him. "Our Lord tells us to repay evil with good," he said. "The day has come for which I have waited so long. Trust in God and he will save us." The Barbarians attacked, and Boniface was the first one killed. He died a martyr on June 5, 754. He was buried at the famous monastery that he had founded at Fulda, Germany. This was what he wanted.

Even today, many people who say they believe in God don't have a true idea of who he is. We can learn more about God by studying our faith, reading the Bible, and having a personal prayer relationship with God our loving Father. Let's also ask St. Boniface to help all those people who have still never heard about Jesus, God's Son.

June 6

St. Norbert

Norbert, the son of Count Heribert, was born in Germany around the year 1080. He was a good boy as a child and teenager. But when he went to live at the court of Emperor Henry V, Norbert really changed. He was anxious to be given positions of honor. He was the first to arrive at parties and celebrations. All he ever thought about was having fun.

Then one day, while Norbert was riding across a field, a sudden storm came up. A flash of lightning struck the ground in front of him. His horse bolted. Norbert was thrown to the ground and knocked unconscious. When he woke, he began to think seriously about the way his life was going. He felt that

God was very near. Norbert realized that the Lord was offering him the grace to change for the better. He decided to become a priest. He was ordained to the priesthood in 1115.

Father Norbert worked hard to make others turn from their worldly ways. He gave everyone a good example by selling all he had to give the money to the poor. Norbert became the founder of a religious congregation for the spreading of the faith. His original group included thirteen men. They lived as a community in the valley of Premontre. That is why they were called Premonstratensians. Today the members are also called Norbertines, in honor of their founder, Norbert.

Norbert was chosen bishop of the city of Magdeburg. He entered the city wearing very poor clothes and no shoes. The porter at the door of the bishop's house didn't know him and refused to let him in. He told the bishop to go and join the other beggars. "But he is our new bishop!" shouted those who knew the saint. The porter was shocked and very sorry. "Never mind, dear brother," Norbert said kindly. "You judge me more correctly than those who brought me here."

Norbert had to clarify a false teaching that denied the real presence of Jesus in the Holy Eucharist. His beautiful words about our Lord's presence in the Blessed Sacrament brought the people back to their holy faith. In March, 1133, Norbert and his great friend, St. Bernard (whose feast is celebrated on

August 20) walked in an unusual procession. When Anacletus II claimed to be the pope, they joined the emperor and his army to accompany the true pope, Innocent II, safely to the Vatican.

Norbert died in 1134. Pope Gregory XIII proclaimed him a saint in 1582.

We can learn many good things from St. Norbert. We can especially learn that the way we live here on earth is preparing us for a life that will never end. St. Norbert also teaches us to love and honor Jesus in the Holy Eucharist.

June 7

Blessed Anne García

Anne, the daughter of peasants, was born in Almendral, Spain, in 1549. She took care of sheep until she was twenty years old. Four miles from her hometown was Avila, the city where St. Teresa and her Carmelite nuns lived. Anne wanted to be a nun too, and St. Teresa accepted her into the monastery. Anne became a lay sister instead of a cloistered nun. This meant that Sister Anne could go out and do the errands while the other nuns who stayed home prayed.

For the last six years of her life, St. Teresa chose Sister Anne to be her traveling companion and secretary. St. Teresa went around to visit the communities of Carmelite nuns. Sometimes she started a new convent. Sometimes she helped the nuns become more enthusiastic about the wonderful life they had chosen. St. Teresa thought very highly of Sister Anne and praised her to the other nuns.

Although Sister Anne never had the chance to go to school, she knew how to read and write. She recorded her experiences with the great St. Teresa. It was Sister Anne who was with her when she died.

Sister Anne's life continued quite normally for six years after St. Teresa's death. Then the superiors decided to open a new convent in Paris, France. Five nuns were selected to go and Sister Anne was one of them. While the people of Paris were warmly greeting the nuns, Sister Anne slipped into the kitchen and prepared a meal for her hungry sisters. Eventually, four of the five nuns moved on to the Netherlands. Sister Anne remained behind in France because she had been appointed the prioress or superior. Considering herself unworthy of this office, she reminded the Lord that most of the young French women joining their community were from rich, noble families. She was only a shepherdess. Within her heart, Sister Anne heard the Lord's answer: "With straws I light my fire."

Sister Anne was later sent to the Netherlands to start more new convents. She went first to Mons and then to Antwerp. The young women who came to join the Carmelites thought of Sister Anne as a saint.

Sister Anne died in Antwerp in 1626. She was proclaimed "blessed" by Pope Benedict XV.

Blessed Anne liked to be in the background. She wasn't ambitious. Whenever we find ourselves wanting to be considered more important than others, we can pray to this holy nun. She will help us concentrate on pleasing God rather than impressing other people.

June 8

St. William of York

William Fitzherbert was born in England in the twelfth century. He was the nephew of King Stephen. As a young man, William was rather easy-going and even a bit lazy. He seems to have given the impression to some that he was not very serious about taking responsibility in life. However, William was very popular with the people of his city of York.

Years later, when the archbishop of York died, William was chosen to take his place. In those times, princes used to interfere in the election of the bishops. This is why many priests did not think William had been properly chosen. It was his uncle, the king, who had appointed him. Even the great St. Bernard persuaded the pope to make someone else archbishop of York. William was asked to step aside because many people felt that his appointment was not valid. William left his bishop's house feeling hurt and humiliated. He went to live with another uncle, a bishop. It seems that William then became a much more spiritual person. He would not accept any of the comforts his uncle offered him. He prayed and performed penances. He began to show how much he cared about his faith and about the Church.

The people of York were angry at what had happened to their archbishop. They could not understand how something like this could take place. There were street fights between those who wanted William and those who did not. Six years passed. William continued to live a quiet life of prayer in the home of his uncle. He asked the Lord for peace for his archdiocese. It did not matter any more if he had been treated unjustly. What mattered was that his people be taken care of.

Finally, his prayers were answered. When the other archbishop died, the pope sent William back to York. He arrived in May, 1154. The people were very happy. But William was an old man by this time, and he died about a month later. He was proclaimed a saint by Pope Honorius III in 1227.

Sometimes people may say things about us that are untrue or exaggerated. When this happens we can ask St. William to help us be as forgiving as he was. We can also ask him to help us not to hold grudges.

June 9

St. Ephrem

Ephrem was born in Mesopotamia around the year 306. He was baptized when he was eighteen. Ephrem eventually went into the hills and became a hermit. He found a cave near the city of Edessa in Syria. He wore patched rags for clothes and he ate what the earth provided.

Ephrem used to become angry easily. But little by little, he gained control over himself. People who met him even thought that he was a very calm person by nature. Ephrem often went to preach in Edessa. He spoke so fervently about God that the people wept. He would tell them that he was a great sinner. He really meant it, too, because although his sins were small, they seemed very big to him. When St. Basil met him, he asked, "Are you Ephrem, the famous servant of Jesus?" Ephrem answered quickly, "I am Ephrem who walks unworthily on the way to salvation." Then Ephrem asked and received advice from St. Basil on how to grow closer to God.

Ephrem spent his time writing spiritual books. He wrote in several languages—Syriac, Greek, Latin and Armenian. His books are so beautiful and spiritual that they have been translated into many languages. They are still read today. Ephrem also wrote hymns for public worship. That is why he is called "the harp of the Holy Spirit." Ephrem's hymns became very popular. As the people sang them, they learned much about the faith. Ephrem died in June of 373. Because he taught so many people through his writings, he was proclaimed a Doctor of the Church many years later in 1920.

When we gather with our parish community for Mass, we can ask St. Ephrem to help us participate as well as we can. An important way to do this is to pray the prayers and responses out loud, and to join in singing the songs.

June 10

Blessed Anna Maria Taigi

Anna Maria was born in Siena, Italy, in 1769. Because her family was poor, they moved to Rome soon after in order to find work. As soon as Anna Maria was old enough, she took a job as a house servant in Rome. There she met another servant named Dominic Taigi. They were married in 1790.

Though the young couple had little income, Anna Maria liked to spend what she could on nice clothes. She was very pretty and she knew it. She spent a lot of time admiring herself in the mirror. But one day, after going to confession, she realized how empty and superficial her life had become. She started to realize that beauty of the soul is the most important thing. So Anna Maria changed her way of living. She began to dress simply and modestly. And she became more prayerful and concerned about others.

Anna Maria and Dominic were blessed with seven children. Three of them died in infancy, but the other four received an excellent upbringing from their mother. In addition to taking care of the needs of her home and family, Anna Maria spent much time in prayer, even while doing her household tasks. She helped those less fortunate than her own family, visiting the hospital and helping to care for the sick. She was an example of Christian virtue to all who knew her.

God blessed Anna Maria with special visions and other spiritual experiences, which she managed to keep hidden from her husband. She felt that Dominic deserved to have a "normal" wife. But many people came to know of her closeness to God and soon she had visitors, even priests and bishops, coming to ask for advice.

Anna Maria Taigi died on June 9, 1837, after forty-eight years of marriage. She was sixty-eight years old. She was beatified in 1920 by Pope Benedict XV.

Blessed Anna Maria Taigi did not become holy because of her visions or her gift of prophecy. What made her a saint was her great love for God and her dedication to her family. Her story proves that people from all walks of life are called to become holy.

St. Barnabas

Although he was not one of the original twelve apostles, Barnabas is called an apostle by St. Luke in the Acts of the Apostles. This is because, like Paul the apostle, Barnabas received a special mission from God. He was a Jew born on the island of Cyprus. His name was Joseph, but the apostles changed it to Barnabas. This name means "son of consolation."

As soon as he became a Christian, Barnabas sold all he owned and gave the money to the apostles. He was a good, kind-hearted man. He was full of enthusiasm to share his belief in and love for Jesus. Barnabas was sent to the city of Antioch to preach the Gospel. Antioch was the third largest city in the Roman Empire. It was where the followers of Jesus were first called Christians. Barnabas realized that he needed help. He thought of Paul of Tarsus, a former persecutor of the Christians who had been converted when Jesus appeared to him. It was Barnabas who convinced St. Peter and the Christian community that Paul really loved Jesus and wanted to spread his Gospel. Barnabas asked Paul to come and work with him. Barnabas was a humble person. He was not afraid of sharing responsibility and power. He knew that Paul, too, had a great gift to give, and he wanted him to have the chance to share that gift.

Sometime later, the Holy Spirit chose Paul and Barnabas for a special assignment. Not long afterward, the two apostles set off on a daring missionary journey. They had many sufferings to bear and often risked their lives. Despite the hardships, their preaching won many people to Jesus and his Church.

Later St. Barnabas went on another missionary journey, this time with his relative, John Mark. They went to Barnabas' own country of Cyprus. So many people became believers through his preaching that Barnabas is called the apostle of Cyprus. It is commonly believed that this great saint was stoned to death in the year 61.

St. Barnabas received a name that symbolized what he was—a good person who encouraged others to love the Lord. Let's always try to cheer up those who are sad or lonely. Let's encourage others to love God by the good example we give.

June 12

St. John Gonzalez de Castrillo

John was born at Sahagún, Spain, in 1419. He received his education from the Benedictine monks of his town. Then John became a parish priest. He could have lived a very comfortable life in the cathedral parish or in other wealthy parishes. But John felt attracted to poverty and the simple lifestyle that Jesus had lived. Father John chose to keep charge only of a small chapel. There he celebrated Mass, preached and taught catechism.

Father John realized that he needed to know theology better. He enrolled in classes at the great Catholic University of Salamanca. After four years of hard study, he became famous as a preacher. Nine years later, he joined a community of Augustinian friars. They were very impressed by the way he practiced the Christian virtues. He was obedient to his superiors and humble, too. He also continued his preaching. His beautiful homilies or sermons brought about a change in the people of Salamanca. They had been quarreling violently among themselves. Often young noblemen fought each other in revenge. Father John succeeded in ending many of these bitter fights. He even persuaded people to forgive one another.

He was not afraid to correct evils, even when the evildoers were powerful people who could take revenge. Once he corrected a duke for the way he was making the poor people suffer. In anger, the duke sent two of his men to kill John. The two men found the priest and approached him. Father John was so calm and kind. Both men were overcome with sorrow and asked his pardon. Then the duke became sick. Through Father John's prayers he repented of his sins and recovered.

It was the graces he received from prayer and from the Mass that gave Father John his special

power as a preacher. He celebrated the Mass with great devotion.

John died on June II, 1479. He was proclaimed a saint by Pope Alexander VIII in 1690.

St. John was a peacemaker because he tried to be loving and kind with everyone. How can we be peacemakers at home or at school?

June 13

St. Anthony of Padua

This very popular saint was born in Lisbon, Portugal, in 1195. His baptismal name was Ferdinand. Ferdinand was taught by the Augustinian friars. When he was old enough, he joined their order. At the age of twenty-five, Ferdinand's life took an exciting turn. He heard about some Franciscans who had been martyred by the Moors in Morocco. These friars were St. Berard and his companions. (We celebrate their feast on January 16.) Ferdinand was so impressed with the courage of the martyrs that he got permission to transfer from the Augustinian Order to the Franciscan Order. This order was very new. St. Francis, its founder, was still alive. Ferdinand took the new name "Anthony." He went off to Africa to preach about Jesus to the Moors. But he soon became so sick that his superiors called him back to

Portugal. On the way there, however, his ship was caught in a terrible storm. It had to land in Italy instead of returning to Portugal.

No one in his new religious order realized how brilliant and talented Anthony was. He never spoke about himself or how much he knew. So the Franciscan superiors assigned him to a quiet friary in Italy. There he washed pots and pans. One day Anthony was unexpectedly asked to preach in front of a crowd of priests and important people. Everyone was surprised at the wonderful things he said about God. From then on, until he died nine years later, Anthony was sent to preach all over Italy. He was so popular that people even closed their stores to go to hear him.

After 1226, Anthony remained in the city of Padua, Italy. There his preaching completely changed the lives of the people. He helped the poor and worked to keep people who couldn't pay their bills from being thrown into prison. His sermons helped people to not only understand their faith better, but to put it into practice, too.

Anthony died at Arcella, near Padua, Italy, on June 13, 1231. He was only thirty-six years old. Pope Gregory IX proclaimed him a saint just one year later.

Many people ask St. Anthony to pray to God for them when they need help. And many miracles have taken place through his intercession. Statues of St. Anthony show him holding the Infant Jesus because Jesus once appeared to him as a baby. Other pictures show St. Anthony holding a Bible. This is because he knew, loved and preached the Word of God so well. In fact, St. Anthony knew Scripture so well that Pope Pius XII proclaimed him the "Evangelical Doctor," or Doctor of Sacred Scripture.

Sometimes we want to be recognized for the things we do well. It may be that we won't always receive as much attention as we would like. That's when we can ask St. Anthony to teach us how to use our gifts without expecting any praise in return.

June 14

St. Andrew Fournet

St. Andrew Fournet was born on December 6, 1752. He was from Maille, a little town near Poitiers, in France. Andrew's parents were religious people. Mrs. Fournet had her heart set on Andrew becoming a priest. The little boy heard this more often than he cared to. Once he declared, "I'm a good boy, but I'm still not going to be a priest or a monk!"

When he grew up, Andrew went to Poitiers to study philosophy and law. But that didn't last long. He was having too much of a good time to study! His mother encouraged him to find good jobs, but they fell through, one after another. Then his mother suggested that Andrew go and stay for a while with his uncle, a holy priest who was living in a poor parish. To his mother's surprise, Andrew agreed.

Andrew's uncle recognized his nephew's good qualities. And the priest's own good example sparked something in Andrew. Andrew began to feel drawn to the priesthood. He started to study seriously to make up for lost time. Andrew was eventually ordained a priest and assigned to be his uncle's assistant. In 1781, he was transferred to his home parish in Maille. His mother was so happy! Andrew had become a caring and prayerful priest.

When the French revolution began, Andrew refused to take an oath that was against the Church. He became a hunted man. In 1792, he was forced to flee to Spain. There he remained for five years. But he worried about his people and went back to France. The danger was as great as before. But Father Andrew was protected by the people. He nearly escaped death several times. Meanwhile, he heard confessions, celebrated the Eucharist, and anointed the sick and dying.

When the Church was free again, Andrew came out of hiding. He was always inviting his people to love and serve God. One of the good ladies from the area, Elizabeth Bichier des Ages (who also became a saint) helped Father Andrew very much. Together they started an order of sisters called the Daughters of the Cross. (St. Elizabeth's feast day is August 26.)

Andrew died on May 13, 1834, at the age of eighty-two. He was proclaimed a saint by Pope Pius XI on June 4, 1933.

Let's ask St. Andrew to help us never to be afraid or ashamed to stand up for what's right.

June 15

St. Germaine of Pibrac

Pibrac is the little village in France where Germaine was born around 1579. She spent her life there. She was a sickly and unattractive girl. In fact, her right hand was deformed and helpless. Her father paid little attention to her. And her stepmother didn't want her around her own healthy children. So Germaine slept in the barn, even in cold weather. She dressed in rags and was laughed at by other children. She spent all day tending the sheep out in the fields. When she came home at night, her stepmother often shouted at her and beat her.

Yet this poor girl learned to talk with God and to remember that he was with her all the time. She always managed to get to daily Mass. She left her sheep in her guardian angel's care. Never once did one wander away from her shepherd's staff, which she would leave standing upright in the ground.

Germaine often gathered young children around her to teach them about the Catholic faith. She wanted their hearts to be full of God's love. She tried her best to help the poor, too. She shared with beggars the little bit of food she was given to eat. One winter day, her stepmother accused her of stealing bread. The woman chased her with a stick. When she finally caught up with Germaine, she demanded to see what Germaine had wrapped in her apron. Her stepmother was amazed to discover not bread but summer flowers!

By now people no longer made fun of Germaine. In fact, they loved and admired her. She could have begun to live in her father's house, but she chose to keep her little corner in the barn. Germaine died in 1601. She was only twenty-two years old. Her life of great suffering was over. And God worked miracles to show everyone that she was a saint.

St. Germaine was very patient in putting up with all the difficulties she had. At Mass and in Holy Communion she received the help she needed from God. Whenever something makes us suffer we should pray for God's help too.

June 16

St. John Francis Regis

This French saint was born in 1597. When he was eighteen, he entered the Jesuit Order. In the seminary, John's love for God and his vocation showed in the way he prayed. He was also eager to teach the faith to people in the parishes whenever he could.

After he was ordained a priest, John Francis began his work as a missionary preacher. He gave very simple talks that came right from his heart. He especially liked to speak to the poor, the ordinary people. They came in great crowds to hear him. Father John Francis spent his mornings praying, celebrating the sacrament of Reconciliation and preaching. In the afternoon, he would visit prisons and hospitals. To someone who said that the prisoners and other sinners he converted would not stay good for long, Father John Francis answered: "If my efforts stop just one sin from being committed, I shall consider them worthwhile."

Father John Francis journeyed to remote mountain parishes even on the coldest days of winter to preach his missions. "I have seen him stand all day on a heap of snow at the top of a mountain preaching," one priest said, "and then spend the whole night hearing confessions." Sometimes he would start off for a far-away town at three o'clock in the morning with a few apples in his pocket for his day's food.

Once, on his way to a village, Father John Francis fell and broke his leg. But he kept on going, leaning on a stick and on his companion's shoulder. When he reached the village, he went at once to hear confessions, without going to see a doctor. At the end of the day, when the doctor finally examined it, his leg was already completely healed! God rewarded the priest's great love with this miracle.

Father John Francis died on one of his preaching missions. He became very ill while lost at night in the woods. Just before he died, he exclaimed: "I see our Lord and his Mother opening heaven for me." He died on December 31, 1640.

In 1806, a pilgrim joined the crowds going to pray at the shrine of St. John Francis Regis. This pilgrim believed all his life that St. John Francis obtained his vocation to the priesthood for him. The pilgrim was St. John Vianney, the Curé of Ars. The Church celebrates his feast on August 4.

The story of St. John Francis shows us what amazing things God can do when we let him work in our lives. Let's pray that God will use us to bring his love to many other people.

June 17

St. Emily de Vialar

Emily de Vialar was an only child. She was born in France in 1797. Her wealthy parents sent her to school in Paris. Fifteen-year-old Emily returned to her small town of Gaillac when her mother died. Her father was interested in finding her a suitable husband. He became angry when Emily refused to marry. Emily knew that she wanted to be a religious sister and give her life to God. But her father was against this idea and used to start arguments to get her to change her mind.

When Emily was twenty-one, a new priest arrived in Gaillac. His name was Father Mercier. He helped Emily to discover that God did want her to serve the poor and the sick. Father Mercier helped her set up an outpatient service right on the terrace of the de Vialar home. Emily's father was upset by all this. This tense situation between Emily and her father lasted for fifteen years. Then Emily's grandfather, the Baron de Portal, died, leaving her a fortune. At last she had the independence she needed to begin her great work for God.

With the help of Father Mercier, Emily bought a large house in her hometown. She and three other women began a religious order. They designed a habit and chose a name. They called themselves the Sisters of St. Joseph of the Apparition. (In Matthew's Gospel, an angel had appeared to Joseph to tell him that Mary's child was from God.) The archbishop blessed their congregation and ministry. These sisters would be dedicated to the care of the sick and poor, and to the education of children. Twelve young women joined the group within three months. Sister Emily pronounced her vows in 1835 along with seventeen other sisters. The archbishop approved the rule they would live by.

The Sisters of St. Joseph opened branch convents. In 1847, some went to Burma and in 1854 other sisters went to Australia. In forty years, Mother Emily saw her congregation grow from the patio of her home in Gaillac, France, to some forty foundations around the world.

Mother Emily wrote many letters that revealed her tremendous love for God, for his Church and for people. She cared about everyone. She saw in her heart people everywhere who needed the truth of the Gospel and the love that Christianity brings. She asked Jesus for the strength she needed to continue on. Mother Emily's health began to fail around 1850. She died in August 1856. Pope Pius XII proclaimed her a saint in 1951.

It's not enough to just believe in the teachings of Jesus. We also have to put them into practice, as St. Emily did. How can you reach out to others? Can you help a friend who's having a hard time with schoolwork? Can you visit elderly people living in a nursing home? How can you help out around the house?

June 18

St. Gregory Barbarigo

Gregory was born in 1625. He was raised and educated in his native city of Venice, Italy. While still in his twenties, Gregory was chosen to go with the Venetian ambassador to Munster, Germany, for the signing of the Treaty of Westphalia on October 24, 1648. This treaty would bring an end to the Thirty Year War. This war, begun in 1618, was fought in

Germany. It involved local, Swedish and French troops and was basically caused by Catholic-Protestant misunderstanding.

At Munster, Gregory met the pope's representative. This man was to become Pope Alexander VII in 1655. He realized the goodness and spiritual qualities of Father Gregory. He made him a bishop and assigned him to the diocese of Bergamo, Italy. In 1660, the pope called Gregory to Rome again. This time he made Gregory a cardinal and assigned him to Padua.

Cardinal Gregory Barbarigo was to spend the rest of his life in that city already made famous by St. Anthony. People often said that Cardinal Barbarigo was like a second Cardinal Borromeo. (We celebrate the feast of St. Charles Borromeo on November 4.)

Cardinal Barbarigo lived a simple, self-sacrificing life. He gave large sums of money to charitable works. He kept his door open and was always available when people were in trouble. He started an excellent college and seminary to train men to be priests. He gave the seminary a wonderful library with many books by the early Church Fathers and books about Sacred Scripture. He even equipped the seminary with a printing press.

Cardinal Gregory Barbarigo died in June, 1697, at the age of seventy-two. He was canonized by Pope John XXIII in 1960.

St. Gregory was always ready to help those who were in trouble. We can imitate him in small ways

*by being kind and welcoming to those who might
not have many friends at school, or by smiling at
someone who looks sad. When we try to treat others as Jesus would we can make a difference.*

June 19

St. Romuald

Romuald, an Italian nobleman, was born around
951 in Ravenna, Italy. When he was twenty, he was
shocked to see his father kill a man in a duel.
Romuald went to a Benedictine monastery. He wanted to set his own life straight. He also wanted to do
penance for his father's drastic deed. The monastery
surroundings and lifestyle were new to Romuald. He
was used to luxury and an easy way of life without
much work. The nobleman was impressed by the
good example of many of the monks. He became a
monk, remaining at the monastery for three years.
After that, he decided to find a stricter way of life. He
asked a good hermit named Marinus to be his spiritual guide. Both Marinus and Romuald tried to spend
each day praising and loving God. Romuald's own
father Sergius came to observe his son's new way of
life. He was struck by its spirit of simplicity and self-
sacrifice. Sergius realized that there had to be great
happiness in this kind of life because his son had
given up everything to live like this. That was all

Sergius needed. He too gave up his wealth and spent the rest of his life as a monk.

Eventually, Romuald began the Camaldolese Benedictine order. He traveled around Italy starting hermitages and monasteries. Wherever he went, he gave his monks a wonderful example of love and penance. He ate very simple meals consisting of food he grew himself. Through these sacrifices Romuald grew closer to God.

Romuald died on June 19, 1027, at the monastery of Valdi-Castro. He was alone in his cell and passed away quietly, probably whispering his favorite prayer: "Oh, my sweet Jesus! God of my heart! Delight of pure souls! The object of all my desires!"

Let's ask St. Romuald to help us to value prayer and the life of Jesus within us. We can also ask him to help us keep our priorities straight. He knows how hard that can sometimes be.

June 20

Blessed Michelina of Pesaro

Michelina was born in 1300 in Pesaro, Italy. Her family was wealthy and she married a rich man. Michelina was a happy person by nature. She and her husband lived a life of luxury and comfort. But when she was just twenty, her husband died. All of a sudden, Michelina found herself alone with a little son to raise.

A holy Franciscan laywoman lived in Pesaro. Her name was Syriaca. Syriaca realized that Michelina was really a wonderful person who needed direction and help to become closer to God. The two women became friends, and Michelina took Syriaca into her home. Michelina was greatly influenced by the holy woman. Michelina became prayerful. She took good care of her son and her home. She spent her free time serving the poor and needy. She visited the lonely and took care of those too sick or too old to look after themselves.

Then, Michelina's son died suddenly. Michelina decided to become a Third Order Franciscan. At first, her relatives were concerned when she gave away her money and fancy clothes and started to eat plain food. But after a while, they became convinced that Michelina was very close to God.

Michelina lived her whole life in the same house in Pesaro. She died in 1356 at the age of fifty-six. In her memory, the people of her town kept a lamp always lit in her home. In 1590, Blessed Michelina's house was made into a church.

Blessed Michelina had the choice to live a selfish, easy life or a life of loving, Christian service. It was through the example of her friend Syriaca that Michelina became holy. Let's thank God for the gift of our own good friends.

St. Aloysius Gonzaga

Aloysius, the patron saint of young Catholics, was born on March 9, 1568 in Castiglione, Italy. Since he was so full of life, his father planned to make a great soldier out of him. When Aloysius was just five, his father took him to the army camp. There, little Aloysius marched in parade. He even managed to load and fire a gun one day while the army was resting. He learned rough language from the soldiers, too. But when he found out what the words meant, Aloysius felt very bad that he had used them.

As he grew, Aloysius was sent to the court of the duke of Mantua. Dishonesty, hatred, and impurity were common there. But the only effect it all had on Aloysius was to make him more careful to live as a good follower of Jesus. He became sick. That gave him an excuse to spend some time praying and reading good books. When Aloysius was sixteen, he decided to become a Jesuit priest. His father refused to allow it. However, after three years, he finally gave in. Once Aloysius had joined the order, he asked to do hard and humble tasks. He served in the kitchen and washed the dishes.

When a terrible sickness called the plague broke out in Rome, Aloysius asked to be allowed to care for the sick. The young man who had grown up with servants waiting on him now washed the sick and made

their beds. He served them until he caught the sickness himself.

Aloysius was only twenty-three years old when he died. It was the night of June 20, 1591. He said simply, "I am going to heaven." The body of Aloysius Gonzaga is buried in the Church of St. Ignatius in Rome. He was proclaimed a saint by Pope Benedict XIII in 1726.

Peer pressure can sometimes make us say and do things that we shouldn't. Let's ask St. Aloysius for the courage to do what's right no matter what others are doing or what they think about us.

June 22

St. John Fisher and St. Thomas More

John Fisher was born in Yorkshire, England, in 1469. He was educated at Cambridge University and became a priest. Father John taught at Cambridge, too. He was a wonderful teacher and helped the students grow in their knowledge of the Catholic faith. But there was a lot of confusion about religion in those days. Father John helped people to know the truth about God and the Catholic Church.

In 1504, he became the bishop of Rochester, England. It was a poor diocese. Bishop John was to remain its shepherd for thirty years. Besides being the bishop of Rochester, he was the head of Cambridge University. Bishop John also heard the confessions of King Henry VIII's mother.

Bishop John had many friends, including the famous scholar, Erasmus, and the great Sir Thomas More. Bishop John and Thomas More would have never guessed that one day they would be sharing a feast day on the calendar of saints!

King Henry VIII became angry with Bishop John for insisting that his marriage to Queen Catherine was true. Then Henry VIII divorced Catherine and married Anne Boleyn in a civil ceremony. The king demanded that people sign an oath of loyalty to him. He made himself head of the Church in England. Bishop John would not sign the oath. He was arrested in 1534 and sent to the Tower of London. The tower was damp and the treatment was harsh. Bishop John suffered very much, but he would not betray his faith. Even though there were no televisions and radios back then, people found out about what Bishop John, Sir Thomas More and others like them were going through. They were shocked and saddened. On June 12, 1535, Pope Paul III named Bishop John a cardinal. He hoped this would make King Henry set him free. But the king only became more angry and mean. After ten months in prison, Cardinal John was beheaded on June 22, 1535.

Along with his friend, Sir Thomas More, Cardinal John Fisher was proclaimed a saint by Pope Pius XI in 1935.

Sometimes it's much easier to go along with the crowd rather than stand up for the truth. But the story of St. John shows that God will always give us the strength we need to do the right thing.

Sir Thomas More was a famous lawyer and writer. He was born in London in 1478. His father had been a lawyer, too, and a judge. Thomas was always grateful to his father for being so loving and for not spoiling him.

Thomas' first wife, Jane Colt, died when she was very young. Thomas was left with four small children. He got married again to a widow named Alice Middleton. She was a good but simple woman who could not even read or write, even though Thomas tried to teach her. Thomas made home life enjoyable for his family because he was so pleasant to be with. During meals, one of the children would read from the Bible. Then they would have fun and tell jokes. Thomas often invited poorer neighbors to come to dinner, too. He always helped the poor as much as he could. He loved to delight his guests with surprises. He even kept some playful monkeys as pets. But few people could have imagined how deeply religious Thomas really was. He prayed long hours into the night and performed penances, too. He was very much aware that he needed the grace and help of God to live as a true Christian.

Thomas held important government positions in England. For three years he was Lord Chancellor, another name for prime minister. King Henry VIII used to put his arm around Thomas' shoulder because they were such good friends. Although Thomas was most loyal to the king, he was loyal to God first of all. In fact, when the king tried to make him disobey God's law, Thomas refused. King Henry wanted to divorce his wife and marry another woman. However, the pope could not give permission, since that is against God's law. Henry was stubborn and at last he left the Church. He wanted everyone to recognize him as the head of the Church in England. Thomas could not do that. He chose to remain faithful to the Catholic faith and to God. He was condemned to death for that, yet he forgave his judges. Thomas even said that he hoped he would see them in heaven. He really meant it, too.

At the scaffold, where he was to die, Thomas declared himself "the king's good servant, but God's first." He kissed his executioner on the cheek. Then he joked, saying that his beard should not be cut off because it had not done anything wrong. Sir Thomas More was martyred on Tuesday, July 6, 1535, at the age of fifty-seven. Sir Thomas More was proclaimed a saint by Pope Pius XI in 1935, together with his friend, Bishop John Fisher. He is the patron saint of lawyers.

St. Thomas risked losing everything: his fortune, his position, his own security and even the safety of his family. But he held fast to his Catholic faith, even to the point of sacrificing his life. Like his friend St. John, Thomas was able to remain strong because he prayed and trusted in God. Let's try to be like him.

St. Paulinus of Nola also shares this feast day with St. John Fisher and St. Thomas More.

June 23

St. Joseph Cafasso

Joseph Cafasso was born in 1811, in northern Italy, near the city of Turin. (In 1815, one of his most famous students John Bosco—who would also become a saint—was born in the same town. We celebrate his feast on January 31.) Joseph had loving parents who, although poor, were willing to sacrifice for his education. When he was old enough, Joseph went to Turin to study to become a priest.

Joseph met John Bosco in 1827 when John was just twelve. The two became friends for the rest of their lives. In 1833, Joseph was ordained a priest. He began his priestly work and went to an excellent school of theology for priests. When Father Joseph graduated, he became a theology professor. He taught many young priests over the years. They could tell that he really loved them.

Father Joseph became known as the priest who believed in the gentle and loving mercy of God.

Because he was so kind himself, he gave people courage and hope. He guided many priests, religious and lay people. He helped John Bosco, who had become Father John Bosco, begin his great work with troubled boys. Father Joseph also guided Father John in starting his religious order known as the Salesians. Father Joseph gave good advice to founders of other religious orders too.

There were many social needs in Father Joseph Cafasso's time. One of the most urgent was the prison system. Prison conditions were terrible. But what most disturbed Father Joseph was the custom of publicly hanging prisoners sentenced to death. Father Joseph went to them and heard their confessions. He stayed with them, telling them of God's love and mercy until they died. He helped over sixty convicted men. All of them repented and died in the peace of Jesus.

No one could ever measure Father Joseph's great influence on people and works in the Church. He died on June 23, 1860. His devoted friend, Father John Bosco, preached the homily at his funeral. Pope Pius XII proclaimed Father Joseph Cafasso a saint in 1947.

We can never be too kind and understanding with people. St. Joseph was especially known for his kindness to those in prison. We may not be able to help those in prison as St. Joseph did, but we can and should pray for them.

June 24

Birth of St. John the Baptist

John's parents were Zachary and Elizabeth. Elizabeth was an elderly cousin of Mary, the mother of Jesus. The archangel Gabriel appeared to Zachary and told him that Elizabeth would have a son, whom he should name John. Zachary doubted the angel, because he and his wife were too old to have children. To show God's power, the angel told Zachary that he would not be able to speak until everything had happened as the Lord had promised.

Later, Gabriel visited Mary and told her that she would become the mother of the Savior. Gabriel also told Mary that Elizabeth was soon to be a mother. Mary went to visit and help her cousin. Then Elizabeth had her baby. Zachary named him John, as the angel had requested. At that moment, Zachary was able to speak again, and he began praising God.

When the neighbors of Zachary and Elizabeth witnessed this, they began to ask each other, "What will this child become?" They knew that God was calling him to something great. John did have a special calling. He was going to prepare the way for the coming of Jesus.

As a young man, John went into the desert to prepare himself for his mission with silence, prayer and penance. Soon crowds started to come to him. They realized he was a holy man. John warned the people to be sorry for their sins. He told them to change their lives, and he gave them the baptism of repentance. That is why he is called John the Baptist. One day, Jesus himself came to John. He wanted to be baptized with John's baptism to begin making up for our sins. On that day, John told the crowds that Jesus was the Messiah, the one they had been waiting for. He told them and everyone else to follow Jesus. John said, "Jesus must become more and more important and I must become less and less important." He said that he was not even worthy to loosen the strap of Jesus' sandal.

We also celebrate the day that John the Baptist was killed by King Herod because that is the day he went to live with Jesus in heaven. This feast is on August 29.

St. John the Baptist was a great prophet. He pointed Jesus out and prepared people to follow Jesus. Let's listen to St. John's advice and allow Jesus to become more and more important in our lives.

June 25

St. William of Vercelli

William was born in Vercelli, Italy, in 1085. His parents died when he was a baby. His relatives raised him. When William grew up, he became a hermit. He worked a miracle, curing a blind man, and found himself famous. William was too humble to be happy with the people's admiration. He really wanted to remain a hermit so that he could concentrate on God. So he went out in the wilderness to live alone on a high mountain. He thought that there no one would bother him. But he was wrong. Many men wanted William to help them become closer to God. They came to live with him, and they built a monastery dedicated to the Blessed Virgin. Because of William's monastery, people gave the mountain a new name. They called it the Mountain of the Virgin.

After a while, some of the monks began to complain that their way of life was too hard. They wanted better food and an easier schedule. William would not relax the rule for himself. Instead, he chose a prior for the monks. Then he and five faithful followers set out to start another monastery, where they could live the strict kind of life they felt called to. One of William's companions was John of Matera. Both William and John were leaders. They realized, as time went on, that it would be better if they split up, and each start a separate monastery. They were great friends, but they saw things differently. So John went east and William went west. Both did very well. In fact, both became saints.

Later, King Roger I of Naples helped William. William's good influence on the king angered some evil men of the court. They tried to prove to the king that William was really evil and that he was hiding behind a holy habit. They sent a woman to tempt William, but she was unsuccessful. It seems that she repented and gave up her life of sin. St. William died on June 25, 1142.

The story of St. William shows that even good friends don't always agree on everything. Even though St. William and St. John had different ideas they didn't let this interfere with their friendship. We can ask St. William to help us to respect the ideas of our friends even when they are different from our own.

June 26

St. Josemaría Escrivá

Josemaría Escrivá was born in Barbastro, Spain, on January 9, 1902. He was one of the six children of José Escrivá and Dolores Balaguer. After he graduated from high school, Josemaría studied law at Saragossa and received his doctorate in Madrid. Then he returned to Saragossa and entered the seminary. After he was ordained a priest on March 28, 1925, Josemaría continued his studies in Rome and earned a doctorate in theology.

Father Escrivá began his priestly ministry in country parishes. Later, he ministered to university students. He worked in the slums of Saragossa and

Madrid, where he came into contact with people from every level of society. He recognized the need to bring the Christian message of faith and hope to the rich and poor, the educated and the simple. In order to fulfill this need, Father Escrivá started an association called *Opus Dei*, which means "the work of God" in Latin. It was an organization for people from all levels of social and professional life who wanted to live the Christian life more fully. Members of *Opus Dei* offer up the work they do each day in union with Jesus. In this way, they make their work, themselves, and others holy.

Father Escrivá traveled throughout Europe and Latin America bringing *Opus Dei* to people in other nations. He taught that everyone is called to live a holy life and to carry out a mission in the Church. He wrote many books on history and law, but his spiritual works were especially popular. His book, *The Way*, which was first published in 1934, has sold over four million copies in over forty languages!

Father Escrivá died suddenly on June 26, 1975, in Rome. At the time of his death, *Opus Dei* had spread to six continents with more than 60,000 members representing eighty nationalities.

Pope John Paul II canonized Father Josemaría Escrivá on October 6, 2002.

St. Josemaría Escrivá taught that the work we do in our everyday lives is a way to become closer to God. When we offer Jesus our schoolwork, our

daily chores, and even our times of fun, our whole
life becomes a prayer and a fulfillment of God's
will. This is what true holiness is.

June 27

St. Cyril of Alexandria

Cyril was born in Alexandria, Egypt, around the
year 370. His uncle, Theophilus, was the patriarch or
archbishop. His uncle meant well, but he had a bad
temper and could be stubborn at times. Archbishop
Theophilus was responsible for sending Bishop John
Chrysostom (who became a saint) into exile in 403.
But the emperor brought the famous bishop back to
his archdiocese of Constantinople. It seems that Cyril
was influenced by his uncle's prejudice of John, and
agreed when Bishop John was sent into exile. (We
celebrate the feast of St. John Chrysostom on
September 13.)

When Theophilus died in 412, Cyril became the
archbishop. He was very clear about his love for the
Church and for Jesus. He was a brave man in confusing times, and he preached what the Church taught.
Cyril was honest and straightforward. He was not
looking for praise or positions. However, Cyril could
be impulsive and stubborn at times. He wanted to
express the truths of the Church with his preaching
and writing, and he did. But when he became upset,

he was not concerned about saying things in a gentle way, so he blurted out angrily at times.

This must have caused him sorrow. Yet Christians were grateful for his many wonderful qualities, such as courage in defending the Church and her teachings.

Cyril was the representative of Pope St. Celestine I at the Council of Ephesus in 431. This was an official Church meeting of over 200 bishops. They had to study the teachings of a priest named Nestorius. The Council explained clearly that Nestorius was wrong about some important truths we believe. For example, he was teaching that Jesus Christ was God, but not man. Of course, Jesus is truly God and truly man. The pope gave Nestorius ten days to promise that he would not keep preaching his errors. But Nestorius would not give in. The Council explained to the people of God that such errors about Jesus could not be accepted. The bishops were so clear in their explanation that these false teachings would never again be a major threat.

The people were very grateful to Cyril of Alexandria who led the Council meetings. Cyril went back to his archdiocese and worked hard for the Church, writing and explaining the truths of the faith until he died in 444. Pope Leo XIII proclaimed St. Cyril a Doctor of the Church in 1882.

It doesn't pay to become discouraged after we've done something that we shouldn't have. What we should do is pray to do better next time. St. Cyril had a hard time controlling his temper, but he kept working on it. Let's ask him to help us become more like Jesus in that virtue that we need the most.

June 28

St. Irenaeus

Irenaeus was a Greek who was born between the years 120 and 140. He had the great privilege of being taught by St. Polycarp, who had been a disciple of St. John the Apostle. Irenaeus once told a friend: "I listened to St. Polycarp's instructions very carefully. I wrote down his actions and his words, not on paper, but on my heart."

After he became a priest, Irenaeus was sent to the French city of Lyons. It was in this city that the bishop, St. Pothinius, was martyred along with a great many other saints. Irenaeus was not martyred at that time because he had left the city to do an errand. His brother priests had asked him to take an important message from them to the pope in Rome. In that letter they spoke of Irenaeus as a man full of zeal for the faith. After reading that letter, the pope made Irenaeus a bishop and sent him back to Lyons.

When Irenaeus returned to Lyons, the persecution was over. But there was another danger—a false religion called Gnosticism was spreading. This false religion attracted some people by its promise to teach them secret mysteries. Irenaeus studied all its teachings and then wrote a five-volume work to explain their errors. He wrote with respect, because he wanted to win people to Jesus. However, sometimes he had to use strong words, too. Many people read Irenaeus' important writings. Before long, the false religion began to die out. St. Irenaeus died around the year 202. Many believe he was martyred.

St. Irenaeus always remembered what he had been taught by St. Polycarp. Let's try to form the habit of being grateful to all those who have taught us many good things: our parents or guardians, our priests and teachers. Let's pray for them and try to put all that we've learned into practice.

June 29

St. Peter and St. Paul

Peter, the first bishop of Rome (we now call the bishop of Rome the pope), was a fisherman from Bethsaida. Jesus invited him to follow him, saying: "I will make you a fisher of people." Peter was a simple, hard-working man. He was generous, honest and very attached to Jesus.

This great apostle's original name was Simon, but Jesus changed it to Peter, which means "rock." "You

are Peter," Jesus said, "and on this rock I will build my Church." Peter was the leader of the apostles.

When Jesus was arrested, Peter became afraid. That's when he denied that he knew Jesus three times. But Peter was very sorry for what he had done, and Jesus forgave him. After his resurrection Jesus asked Peter three times, "Do you love me?" "Lord," Peter answered, "you know all things. You know that I love you." Peter was right. Jesus really did know! Jesus said kindly, "Feed my lambs. Feed my sheep." Jesus was telling Peter to take care of his Church because he would be ascending into heaven. Jesus made Peter the leader of his followers.

Peter eventually went to live in Rome. Rome was the center of the whole world at that time. Peter converted many nonbelievers there. When the fierce persecution of Christians began, they begged Peter to leave Rome and save himself. There is a tradition that says Peter actually started to run away. But he met Jesus on the road. "Lord, where are you going?" Peter asked him. Jesus answered, "I am going to Rome to be crucified a second time." Then Peter turned around and went back. He realized that this vision meant that he was to suffer and die for Jesus. Soon after, he was taken prisoner and condemned to death. Because he was not a Roman citizen, he, like Jesus, could be crucified. This time he did not deny the Lord. This time he was ready to die for him. Peter asked to be crucified with his head downward since he was not worthy to suffer as Jesus had. The Roman soldiers did not find this unusual because slaves were frequently crucified in the same manner.

St. Peter was martyred and buried on Vatican Hill. It was around the year 67. Emperor Constantine built a large church over that holy spot in the fourth century. Today the beautiful church called St. Peter's Basilica stands there.

St. Peter has another feast that we celebrate. It is on February 22 and is called the Chair of St. Peter.

We can learn from St. Peter that when we make Jesus the center of our hearts and lives everything else will work out. Our sins and failings will never keep Jesus from loving and forgiving us.

Saul was Jewish, but because he was born in Tarsus, he was also a Roman citizen, with the Roman name "Paul." He studied his Jewish faith carefully and was very dedicated to it. Saul made his living as a tentmaker.

Before Saul's conversion, he thought he was pleasing God by persecuting the Christians. At the time of his conversion, Jesus had said: "I will show him how much he must suffer for me." After Jesus appeared to Saul, Saul began to use his Roman name Paul. Paul loved Jesus very much, so much, in fact, that he tried to imitate him in every way. All his life, during his many missionary trips, Paul met troubles and went through dangers of every kind. He was whipped, stoned, shipwrecked, and lost at sea. Many, many times he was hungry, thirsty and cold. But Paul always trusted in God. And he never stopped preaching. "The love of Jesus presses me onward," he said. In reward, God gave him great comfort and joy in spite of every suffering.

We read about St. Paul's marvelous adventures for Jesus in St. Luke's Acts of the Apostles, beginning with chapter nine. But St. Luke's story ends when Paul arrives in Rome. He is under house arrest, waiting to be tried by Emperor Nero. A famous early Christian writer, Tertullian, tells us that Paul was freed after his first trial. But then he was put in prison again. This time he was sentenced to death. He died around the year 67, during Nero's terrible persecution of the Christians.

Paul called himself the apostle of the Gentiles because he preached the Gospel to the people who weren't Jewish. That took him across the then-known world. Because of Paul, we too, have received the Christian faith. In the New Testament, we can read many of the letters which he wrote to the churches which he helped form. In these letters, St. Paul gives helpful advice on living the Christian life.

We celebrate another feast of St. Paul, the feast of his conversion, on January 25.

Once St. Paul discovered who Jesus was, he dedicated his whole life to loving and serving the Lord and telling as many people as he could about him. What can we do to help others know Jesus better?

June 30

First Martyrs of the Church of Rome

The people we honor today had one thing in common: they all gave up their lives for Jesus. They were killed because they were his followers. By the year 64, Emperor Nero's human rights violations had reached proportions beyond description. When a fire broke out in Rome on July 16, it was commonly believed that the emperor himself had set it. As almost the entire city lay in ruins, the anger of the people grew. Nero became fearful. He needed to blame the fire on someone else, and he picked the Christians.

Tacitus, a well-known historian, recorded that the Christians suffered cruel deaths. Nero had some of them fed to wild animals. Others were tied to posts and became human torches that lit the Roman streets. The exact number of these Christian heroes is not known, but their gift of witness and their holy lives made a lasting impact on the people. Nero was the first Roman emperor to persecute the Christians, but he was not the last. And the more the Church was persecuted, the more it grew. The martyrs had paid the price so that all who would come after them would be free to practice the Catholic faith.

We can be grateful that we live in a country in which we are free to practice our Catholic faith. Many other people do not have this same gift. Let's ask the Martyrs of Rome to help all those who are persecuted because of their faith in Jesus.

Index

Alphabetical Listing by First Name of the Saints and Blesseds Featured in Volumes 1 and 2

A

St. Adalbert *April 23*

St. Adelaide *December 16* (volume 2)

St. Adrian of Canterbury *January 9*

St. Agatha *February 5*—Patroness of the Island of Malta and of nurses

St. Agnes *January 21*—Patroness of chastity, of the Children of Mary, and the Girl Scouts

St. Agnes of Bohemia *March 2*

St. Agnes of Montepulciano *April 20*

St. Aiden of Lindisfarne *August 31* (volume 2)

St. Albert the Great *November 15* (volume 2)— Patron of medical technicians and scientists

All Saints' Day *November 1* (volume 2)

All Souls' Day *November 2* (volume 2)

St. Aloysius Gonzaga *June 21*—Patron of youth

St. Alphonsus Liguori *August 1* (volume 2)— Patron of confessors

St. Alphonsus Rodriguez *October 30* (volume 2)

St. Anthony of Egypt *January 17*—Patron of gravediggers, butchers, basket and brush makers

St. Anthony of Padua *June 13*—Patron of finding lost articles, the poor, childless married women, and cemetery workers

Blessed Antoine Frédéric Ozanam *April 10*

St. Apollinarus *July 20* (volume 2)

St. Apollonia and the Martyrs of Alexandria *February 9*—Patroness of dentists and prayed to for toothaches

Assumption of the Blessed Virgin Mary *August 15* (volume 2)

St. Athanasius *May 2*

St. Augustine *August 28* (volume 2)—Patron of theologians, printers, and brewers

St. Augustine of Canterbury *May 27*—Patron of England

St. Augustine Zhao Rong and Companions *July 9* (volume 2)

B

St. Barachisius and St. Jonas *March 29*

St. Barbatus *February 19*

St. Barnabus *June 11*

St. Bartholomew *August 24* (volume 2)—Patron of plasterers

Blessed Bartolo Longo *October 3* (volume 2)

St. Basil and St. Gregory Nazianzen *January 2*—St. Basil: Patron of hospital administrators

St. Bede the Venerable *May 25*

Beheading of St. John the Baptist *August 29* (volume 2)

St. Benedict *July 11* (volume 2)—Co-patron of Europe with St. Cyril and St. Methodius; patron of monks and protector against poisoning

St. Benedict Joseph Labre *April 16*—Patron of homeless people

St. Berard and Companions *January 16*

St. Bernard of Corleone *January 11*

St. Bernard *August 20* (volume 2)—Patron of candlemakers

St. Bernardine of Siena *May 20*—Patron of advertisers, media personnel; people in public relations and prayed to by, or for, people addicted to gambling

St. Bertilla *November 5* (volume 2)

Blessed Bertrand of Garrigues *September 6* (volume 2)

St. Bibiana *December 2* (volume 2)

Birth of the Blessed Virgin Mary *September 8* (volume 2)

Birth of St. John the Baptist *June 24*

St. Blase *February 3*—Patron and protector against throat ailments

St. Bonaventure *July 15* (volume 2)

St. **Boniface** *June 5*—Patron of Germany

St. **Bridget of Sweden** *July 23* (volume 2)—Patroness of Sweden

St. **Brigid of Ireland** *February 1*—Patroness of Ireland, of newborn babies, and dairy workers

C

St. **Caesarius of Nazianzen** *February 25*

St. **Cajetan** *August 7* (volume 2)

St. **Callistus I** *October 14* (volume 2)

St. **Camillus de Lellis** *July 18* (volume 2)

St. **Casimir** *March 4*—Patron of Poland

St. **Catherine Labouré** *November 28* (volume 2)

St. **Catherine of Alexandria** *November 25* (volume 2)—Patroness of philosophers, jurists, teachers, students, and wheel-makers

St. **Catherine of Ricci** *February 13*

St. **Catherine of Siena** *April 29*—Patroness of Italy, of nurses, and of fire prevention

Blessed **Catherine of St. Augustine** *May 8*

St. **Cecilia** *November 22* (volume 2)—Patroness of musicians, poets, singers, and organ builders

Blessed **Ceferino Giménez Malla** *May 4*

St. **Celestine V** *May 19*—Patron of bookbinders

Chair of St. Peter *February 22*

St. **Charles Borromeo** *November 4* (volume 2)—Patron of catechists

St. Charles Lwanga and Companions *June 3*—St. Charles Lwanga: Patron of black African children

Christmas *December 25* (volume 2)

Blessed Christina Ciccarelli *January 18*

St. Christopher Magallanes *May 21*

St. Clare *August 11* (volume 2)—Patroness of television

St. Colette *March 6*

Blessed Contardo Ferrini *October 27* (volume 2)—Patron of universities

Conversion of St. Paul *January 25*

St. Cornelius and St. Cyprian *September 16* (volume 2)

St. Cosmas and St. Damian *September 26* (volume 2)—Patrons of surgeons, barbers, doctors, and pharmacists

St. Cuthbert *March 20*—Patron of sailors

St. Cyril and St. Methodius *February 14*—Co-patrons of Europe, along with St. Benedict

St. Cyril of Alexandria *June 27*

St. Cyril of Jerusalem *March 18*

St. Cyprian and St. Cornelius *September 16* (volume 2)

D

St. Damasus I *December 11* (volume 2)

St. Damian and St. Cosmas *September 26* (volume 2)—Patrons of surgeons, barbers, doctors, and pharmacists

St. Damien Joseph de Veuster of Molokai
May 10

St. David of Wales *March 1*

Dedication of the Basilica of St. Mary Major
August 5 (volume 2)

Dedication of the Basilica of St. John Lateran
November 9 (volume 2)

St. Deogratias *March 22*

Blessed Diego *March 24*

St. Dominic *August 8* (volume 2)—Patron of astronomers

St. Dominic of Silos *December 20* (volume 2)

St. Dominic Savio *March 10*—Patron of choir boys

E

St. Edith Stein *August 9* (volume 2)

St. Edmund *November 20* (volume 2)

St. Edmund Campion *December 1* (volume 2)

St. Edward *October 13* (volume 2)

The Eleven Martyrs of Almeria, Spain *October 26* (volume 2)

Blessed Elisabetta Canori-Mora *February 18*

St. Elizabeth Ann Seton *January 4*

St. Elizabeth Bichier *August 26* (volume 2)

St. Elizabeth of Hungary *November 17* (volume 2)—Patroness of third order members, of bakers, soup kitchens, and shelters

St. Elizabeth of Portugal *July 4* (volume 2)

St. Emily de Vialar *June 17*

St. Ephrem *June 9*

St. Eugene de Mazenod *May 29*

Blessed Eugene III *July 8* (volume 2)

Exaltation of the Holy Cross *September 14* (volume 2)

F

St. Fabian and St. Sebastian *January 20*

St. Faustinus and St. Jovita *February 15*— Patrons of the city of Brescia

St. Felicity and St. Perpetua *March 7*— St. Felicity: Patroness of motherhood

St. Felix of Cantalice *May 16*

St. Fiacre *August 30* (volume 2)

St. Fidelis of Sigmaringen *April 24*

First Martyrs of the Church of Rome *June 30*

St. Frances of Rome *March 9*—Patroness of motorists, along with St. Christopher

St. Frances Xavier Cabrini *November 13* (volume 2)—Patroness of immigrants, emigrants, and hospital administrators

St. Francis Anthony of Lucera *November 29*

St. Francis Borgia *October 10* (volume 2)

St. Francis Caracciolo *June 4*

St. Francis de Sales *January 24*—Patron of authors, journalists, and the deaf

St. Francis of Assisi *October 4* (volume 2)— Patron of Italy, of Catholic Action, of merchants, ecologists and animals

St. Francis of Paola *April 2*—Patron of seamen

St. Francis Xavier *December 3* (volume 2)— Patron of missionaries, the Apostleship of Prayer, Borneo, Australia, New Zealand, and China

St. Francois de Montmorency Laval *May 6*

G

St. Gabriel, St. Michael, St. Raphael, Archangels *September 29* (volume 2)— St. Gabriel: Patron of radio, television, telephone workers, and mail carriers

St. Gabriel Possenti *February 27*—Patron of seminarians and youth

St. Gemma Galgani *March 11*

St. Genevieve *January 29*—Patroness of Paris

St. Germaine of Pibrac *June 15*—Patroness of sheepherders

St. Gianna Beretta Molla *April 27*

St. Giles *September 1* (volume 2)—Patron of the handicapped, homeless, and blacksmiths

St. Giles Mary *February 7*

Blessed Giuseppe Antonio Tovini *November 7* (volume 2)

St. Isaac Jogues, St. John de Brebeuf, and Companions *October 19* (volume 2)

St. Isidore of Seville *April 4*

St. Isidore the Farmer *May 15*—Patron of farmers

J

Blessed James Alberione *November 26* (volume 2)

St. James and St. Philip *May 3*

Blessed James Duckett *April 19*

St. James the Greater *July 25* (volume 2)

St. Jane Frances de Chantal *August 18 in U.S.A.* (volume 2)—Patroness of hunters

St. Jane Valois *February 4*

St. Januarius *September 19* (volume 2)—Patron of bloodbanks

St. Jerome *September 30* (volume 2)—Patron of librarians

St. Joachim and St. Ann *July 26* (volume 2)— St. Joachim: Patron of grandfathers

St. Joan Delanoe *August 17* (volume 2)

St. Joan of Arc *May 30*—Patron of France, of virgins, servicewomen, and soldiers

St. John the Apostle *December 27* (volume 2)— Patron of Asia Minor

St. John Baptist de la Salle *April 7*—Patron of teachers

St. John Baptist Rossi *May 23*

St. John Berchmans *November 27* (volume 2)—Patron of students and altar boys

St. John Bosco *January 31*—Patron of editors and laborers

St. John of Capistrano *October 23* (volume 2)—Patron of jurists and military chaplains

St. John Chrysostom *September 13* (volume 2)—Patron of preachers

St. John Climacus *March 30*

St. John of Damascus *December 4* (volume 2)

St. John de Brebeuf, St. Isaac Jogues, and Companions *October 19* (volume 2)

Blessed John Duckett and Blessed Ralph Corby *September 7* (volume 2)

St. John DuLau and the September Martyrs *September 2* (volume 2)

St. John Eudes *August 19* (volume 2)

St. John Fisher and St. Thomas More *June 22*

St. John Francis Regis *June 16*—Patron of medical social workers

St. John I *May 18*

St. John Gaulbert *July 12* (volume 2)—Patron of forest workers

St. John Gonzalez de Castrillo *June 12*

St. John Joseph of the Cross *March 5*

St. John Leonardi *October 9* (volume 2)

St. John Mary Vianney *August 4* (volume 2)—Patron of parish priests

St. John Neumann *January 5*

St. John of Egypt *March 27*

St. John of God *March 8*—Patron of hospitals, the sick, heart patients,of nurses, and booksellers

St. John of Kanty *December 23* (volume 2)

St. John of the Cross *December 14* (volume 2)

St. John Roberts *December 10* (volume 2)

St. John the Almsgiver *January 10*

St. John XXIII *October 20* (volume 2)

St. Jonas and St. Barachisius *March 29*

St. Josaphat *November 12* (volume 2)

Blessed Josefa Naval Girbes *February 24*

St. Josemaría Escrivá *June 26*

St. Joseph, Husband of Mary *March 19*—Patron of the Universal Church, the dying, families, carpenters, providing for spiritual and physical needs

St. Joseph Cafasso *June 23*—Patron of prisoners

St. Joseph Cupertino *September 18* (volume 2)—Patron of aviators

St. Joseph Moscati *April 12*

St. Joseph the Worker *May 1*

St. Josephine Bakhita *February 8*—Patron of workers

St. Jovita and St. Faustinus *February 15*—Patrons of the city of Brescia

St. Juan Diego *December 9* (volume 2)

St. Jude and St. Simon *October 28* (volume 2)—
St. Jude: Patron of impossible, desperate cases
and of hospitals

St. Julie Billiart *April 8*

St. Junípero Serra *July 1* (volume 2)

St. Justin *June 1*—Patron of philosophers

K

St. Kateri Tekakwitha *July 14* (volume 2)—
Patroness of Native Americans

St. Katharine Drexel *March 3*

St. Kenneth *October 11* (volume 2)

L

St. Lawrence *August 10* (volume 2)—Patron of
cooks and the poor

St. Lawrence of Brindisi *July 21* (volume 2)

**Blessed Lawrence Humphrey, Blessed Roger
Dickenson, and Blessed Ralph Milner**
July 7 (volume 2)

St. Lawrence Justinian *September 11* (volume 2)

St. Lawrence O'Toole *November 14* (volume 2)

St. Lawrence Ruiz and Companions *September 28* (volume 2)

St. Leo IV *July 17* (volume 2)

St. Leo the Great *November 10* (volume 2)

St. Lidwina *April 22*—Patroness of skaters

St. **Louis of France** *August 25* (volume 2)—
Patron of third order members and of barbers

St. **Lucy** *December 13* (volume 2)—Patroness of
people with eye diseases

St. **Luke** *October 18* (volume 2)—Patron of medical doctors, painters, glass-workers, and brewers

St. **Lupicinus and St. Romanus** *February 28*

M

St. **Macrina the Elder** *January 14*

St. **Madeline Sophie Barat** *April 9*

Blessed **Magdalene Martinengo** *July 28* (volume 2)

Blessed **Marcel Callo** *April 19*

St. **Marcellinus and St. Peter** *June 2*

St. **Margaret Clitherow** *March 26*

St. **Margaret Mary Alacoque** *October 16* (volume 2)—Apostle of the Sacred Heart

St. **Margaret of Cortona** *February 20*

St. **Margaret of Scotland** *November 16* (volume 2)—Patroness of learning

St. **Marguerite Bourgeoys** *January 12*

St. **Marguerite d'Youville** *December 22* (volume 2)

St. **Maria Faustina Kowalska** *October 5* (volume 2)

St. **Maria Goretti** *July 6* (volume 2)—Patroness of
virgins, of chastity and of the Children of Mary

St. **Maria Soledad Torres-Acosta** *January 30*

St. **Mariana of Quito** *May 28*

St. **Marianne Cope** *January 23*

Blessed Marie-Leonie Paradis *May 24*

St. Marie of the Incarnation *April 18*

Blessed Marie Rose Durocher *October 6* (volume 2)

St. Mark the Evangelist *April 25*—Patron of notaries

St. Martha *July 29* (volume 2)—Patroness of cooks, domestic servants, hospital dietitians, and innkeepers

St. Martin de Porres *November 3* (volume 2)—Patron of Black Americans and hairdressers

St. Martin I *April 13*

St. Martin of Tours *November 11* (volume 2)—Patron of the homeless and of soldiers

St. Mary di Rosa *December 15* (volume 2)

St. Mary Magdalene *July 22* (volume 2)

Blessed Mary Magdalen Martinengo *July 28* (volume 2)

St. Mary Mazzarello *May 5*

Mary, Mother of God *January 1*

St. Matthew *September 21* (volume 2)—Patron of bankers, tax collectors, and accountants

St. Matilda *March 14*

St. Matthias *May 14*

St. Maximilian Kolbe *August 14* (volume 2)

St. Meletius *February 12*

St. Methodius and St. Cyril *February 14*—Co-patrons of Europe, along with St. Benedict

St. Michael, St. Raphael, St. Gabriel, Archangels *September 29* (volume 2)— St. Michael: Patron of France, of radiologists, persons in battle, paratroopers, grocers, mariners, and helper in temptation

Blessed Michelina of Pesaro *June 20*

Blessed Miguel Augustin Pro *November 23* (volume 2)

St. Monica *August 27* (volume 2)—Patroness of mothers and converts

Most Holy Name of Jesus *January 3*

Most Holy Name of the Blessed Virgin Mary *September 12* (volume 2)

N

St. Narcissus *October 29* (volume 2)

St. Nicholas *December 6* (volume 2)—Patron of children, sailors, bakers, merchants, prisoners, Greece, and co-patron with St. Andrew of Russia

Blessed Nicholas Albergati *May 9*

St. Nicholas of Tolentino *September 10* (volume 2)—Patron of mariners

St. Norbert *June 6*

Blessed Notker *April 6*

O

St. Oliver Plunket *July 2* (volume 2)

St. **Olympias** *December 17* (volume 2)

St. **Onesimus** *February 16*

Our Lady of Fatima *May 13*

Our Lady of Guadalupe *December 12* (volume 2)—Patroness of Mexico, Latin America, and the Philippines

Our Lady of Lourdes *February 11*

Our Lady of Mount Carmel *July 16* (volume 2)

Our Lady of Sorrows *September 15* (volume 2)

Our Lady of the Rosary *October 7* (volume 2)

P/Q

St. **Pancras** *May 12*

St. **Paschal Baylon** *May 17*—Patron of Eucharistic congresses and Eucharistic societies

St. **Patrick** *March 17*—Patron of Ireland

St. **Paul** *January 25/June 29*—Patron of Malta, of journalists, and of hospital public relations

St. **Paul and St. Peter** *June 29*

St. **Paul Chŏng Hasang and St. Andrew Kim Taegŏn** *September 20* (volume 2)

St. **Paul Miki and Companions** *February 6*

St. **Paul the Hermit** *January 15*—Patron of weavers

St. **Paula** *January 19*

St. **Perpetua and St. Felicity** *March 7*

St. **Peter and St. Marcellinius** *June 2*

St. **Peter and St. Paul** *June 29*—St. Peter: Patron of fishermen

St. Peter Canisius *December 21* (volume 2)—
Patron of Germany

St. Peter Chanel *April 28*

St. Peter Chrysologus *July 30* (volume 2)

St. Peter Claver *September 9* (volume 2)—Patron
of Colombia and of Black Catholic missions

St. Peter Damian *February 21*

St. Peter Julian Eymard *August 2* (volume 2)

St. Peter Nolasco *December 24* (volume 2)

Blessed Peter ToRot *July 19* (volume 2)

St. Philip and St. James *May 3*

St. Philip Benizi *August 3* (volume 2)

St. Philip Howard *November 8* (volume 2)

St. Philip Neri *May 26*—Patron of Rome and of
teenagers

Blessed Pier Giorgio Frassati *July 8* (volume 2)

St. Pio of Pietrelcina *September 23* (volume 2)

St. Pius V *April 30*

St. Pius X *August 21* (volume 2)

St. Polycarp *February 23*

St. Pontian and St. Hippolytus *August 13*
(volume 2)

St. Porphyry *February 26*

Presentation of Mary *November 21* (volume 2)

Presentation of the Lord *February 2*

Queenship of Mary *August 22* (volume 2)

R

Blessed Ralph Corby and Blessed John Duckett *September* 7 (volume 2)

Blessed Ralph Milner, Blessed Roger Dickenson, and Blessed Lawrence Humphrey *July* 7 (volume 2)

St. Raphael, St. Michael, St. Gabriel, Archangels *September 29* (volume 2)—St. Raphael: Patron of blind people, of doctors, nurses, lovers, travelers, and happy endings

St. Raymond of Peñafort *January* 7—Patron of Church lawyers and of librarians of medical records

St. Richard de Wyche *April 3*

Blessed Richard Gwyn *October 25* (volume 2)

St. Rita of Cascia *May 22*—Patroness of impossible cases

St. Robert Bellarmine *September 17* (volume 2)— Patron of catechists

Blessed Roger Dickenson, Blessed Roger Milner, and Blessed Lawrence Humphrey *July* 7 (volume 2)

St. Romanus and St. Lupicinus *February 28*

St. Romuald *June 19*

St. Rose of Lima *August 23* (volume 2)— Patroness of the Americas, the Philippines, and the West Indies

St. Rose of Viterbo *September 4* (volume 2)

St. Rose Philippine Duchesne *November 18* (volume 2)

St. Rose Venerini *May 7*

S

St. Sabas *December 5* (volume 2)

St. Scholastica *February 10*—Patroness and protector against convulsions in children

St. Sebastian and St. Fabian *January 20*—Patron of athletes and archers

St. Seraphim of Montegranero *October 12* (volume 2)

St. Seraphina *March 13*

St. Serapion *March 21*

St. Sergius *September 25* (volume 2)

Seven Founders of the Order of Servites *February 17*

St. Sharbel Makhlouf *July 24* (volume 2)

St. Simeon *October 8* (volume 2)

St. Simon and St. Jude *October 28* (volume 2)

St. Sixtus II *August 7* (volume 2)

St. Stanislaus Kostka *August 12* (volume 2)

St. Stanislaus *April 11*—Patron of Poland and of receiving the Anointing of the Sick

St. Stephen *December 26* (volume 2)—Patron of stonemasons and bricklayers

St. Stephen Harding *April 17*

St. Stephen of Hungary *August 16* (volume 2)—Patron of Hungary

St. Sylvester *December 31* (volume 2)

T

St. **Teresa of Avila** *October 15* (volume 2)—
Protector against headaches

Blessed Teresa of Calcutta *September 5* (volume 2)

St. **Thecla** *September 24* (volume 2)

St. **Theophane Venard** *November 6* (volume 2)

St. **Thérèse of the Child Jesus** *October 1* (volume 2)—Patroness of missionaries, of tuberculosis patients, aviators, and florists

St. **Thomas the Apostle** *July 3* (volume 2)—
Patron of the East Indies and of architects

St. **Thomas Aquinas** *January 28*—Universal patron of universities, colleges, and schools

St. **Thomas Becket** *December 29* (volume 2)

St. **Thomas More and St. John Fisher** *June 22*—
St. Thomas More: Patron of lawyers

St. **Thomas of Villanova** *September 22* (volume 2)

St. **Timothy and St. Titus** *January 26*—
St. Timothy: Patron and protector against stomach disorders

Blessed Timothy Giaccardo *October 22* (volume 2)—Patron of media evangelizers

Blessed Titus Brandsma *July 27* (volume 2)

St. **Titus and St. Timothy** *January 26*—St. Titus: Patron of Crete

Blessed Torello *March 16*

Transfiguration of the Lord *August 6* (volume 2)

Who are the Daughters of St. Paul?

We are Catholic sisters.
Our mission is to be
like Saint Paul and tell
everyone about Jesus!
There are so many ways
for people to communicate
with each other. We want
to use all of them so
everyone will know how
much God loves them. We
do this by printing books
(you're holding one!),
making radio shows,
singing, helping people at
our bookstores, using the
Internet, and in many other
ways.

Visit our website at www.pauline.org

BOOKS & MEDIA

The Daughters of St. Paul operate book and media centers at the following addresses. Visit, call, or write the one nearest you today, or find us at www.pauline.org.

CALIFORNIA

3908 Sepulveda Blvd, Culver City, CA 90230	310-397-8676
935 Brewster Avenue, Redwood City, CA 94063	650-369-4230
5945 Balboa Avenue, San Diego, CA 92111	858-565-9181

FLORIDA

145 S.W. 107th Avenue, Miami, FL 33174	305-559-6715

HAWAII

1143 Bishop Street, Honolulu, HI 96813	808-521-2731

ILLINOIS

172 North Michigan Avenue, Chicago, IL 60601	312-346-4228

LOUISIANA

4403 Veterans Memorial Blvd, Metairie, LA 70006	504-887-7631

MASSACHUSETTS

885 Providence Hwy, Dedham, MA 02026	781-326-5385

MISSOURI

9804 Watson Road, St. Louis, MO 63126	314-965-3512

NEW YORK

64 W. 38th Street, New York, NY 10018	212-754-1110

SOUTH CAROLINA

243 King Street, Charleston, SC 29401	843-577-0175

TEXAS

Currently no book center; for parish exhibits or outreach evangelization, contact: 210-569-0500 or SanAntonio@paulinemedia.com

VIRGINIA

1025 King Street, Alexandria, VA 22314	703-549-3806

CANADA

3022 Dufferin Street, Toronto, ON M6B 3T5	416-781-9131

¡También somos su fuente para libros,
videos y música en español!